A Childhood in Malabar
A Memoir

Kamala Das

Translated from the Malayalam
by Gita Krishnankutty

PENGUIN BOOKS

Penguin Books India (P) Ltd., 11 Community Centre, Panchsheel Park, New Delhi 110017, India
Penguin Books Ltd., 80 Strand, London WC2R 0RL, UK
Penguin Group Inc., 375 Hudson Street, New York, NY 10014, USA
Penguin Books Australia Ltd., 250 Camberwell Road, Camberwell, Victoria 3124, Australia
Penguin Books Canada Ltd., 10 Alcorn Avenue, Suite 300, Toronto, Ontario, M4V 3B2, Canada
Penguin Books (NZ) Ltd., Cnr Rosedale & Airborne Roads, Albany, Auckland, New Zealand
Penguin Books (South Africa) (Pty) Ltd., 24 Sturdee Avenue, Rosebank 2196, South Africa

Originally published in Malayalam in two volumes as *Balyakala Smaranakal* (Memories of Childhood) by D.C. Books, Kottayam, 1987 and *Varshangalkku Mumbu* (Many Years Ago) by Current Books, Thrissur, 1989.

First published by Penguin Books India 2003

Copyright © Kamala Das 2003
This translation copyright © Penguin Books India 2003

10 9 8 7 6 5 4 3 2 1

Typeset in Sabon by S.R. Enterprises, New Delhi
Printed at Baba Barkhanath Printers, New Delhi

Preface

Ramanlal Patel, a psychoanalyst of great repute, was my good friend and used to send many of his younger patients to me. I would coax them to draw pictures or try to put their thoughts into words. As they did this, they would gradually begin to feel better, to readjust to the business of living.

One day, I accompanied another friend of mine who was going to consult Ramanlal. Watching her lie on the couch and speak to him, I wanted to speak to him too. He asked me to lie on the couch and go as far back in time as I could and tell him my very first memory . . .

The image that I recalled was that of a bare-breasted woman standing at a great height, on the roof of a huge building, dangling me over the low wall of the terrace. I could hear the muted roar of the traffic in the street below as she threatened to throw me down if I did not stop crying. As the image grew sharper, I remembered that I had always suffered from vertigo.

'Wonderful,' cried Ramanlal, 'that could well be your first memory.' He asked me to try to find out whether something like what I had described had actually happened. My mother told me that when I was about a year and a half old, we used to live in a red, three-storeyed house on Rashbihari Avenue in Calcutta. My parents had brought a woman from Kerala to look after me, a middle-aged woman named Marath Chinnu Amma, who never wore blouses and preferred to leave her breasts uncovered, as was the custom then prevalent in Kerala.

Piecing together the bits and pieces I could describe of this memory, Amma said that Chinnu Amma could well have threatened me as I recalled since she often used to take me up to the terrace of our house. My father was ill at the time with typhoid and Chinnu Amma probably did not want me to disturb him.

Ramanlal urged me to exercise my memory, to make a deliberate effort to recall people, events, experiences and, most importantly, bits of dialogue from the distant past, from my childhood. Exploring the memory, he said, could be a very exciting and rewarding task. He and his wife Padmaben began to visit me every Saturday. They would bring me a packet of Bourbon biscuits filled with chocolate cream and we would spend our time dredging the past, laughing over the people and incidents I recalled. As memory after memory surfaced, accompanied by fragments of speech, I felt them explode within me like a shower of fireworks, lighting up forgotten areas of my life, filling them with colour and sound and scent.

Often, I would grow physically tired with the effort of remembering and the weight of memory would prove too heavy a burden for me as I journeyed through a childhood in which I had shuttled between Calcutta and Malabar, shifting between three different cultures: of Kerala where I used to spend the long summer holidays, of Calcutta where I lived with my parents and the British culture I encountered at St Cecilia's, the school I went to while we were in Calcutta. I slowly learned to sort out these memories, to find words for them, to arrange them in some kind of sequence. The first volume that poured out of this exercise was *Memories of Childhood*; *Many Years Ago* soon followed.

Yesterdays

I still remember very clearly the day Ammamma first took me to the kovilakam, the palace where the Thampurans lived. That was the day I first learned about the caste system.

I remember the two granite statues at the gate of the kovilakam. Ammamma told me they were sentries. I thought fondly of the uniformed watchman who stood at the gate of the house in Calcutta where my parents lived, on Park Street. A live doorkeeper! And a dear friend, who always let me sit with him on his charpoi and asked me questions about my teacher and my ayah.

Ammamma held my hand tight as we entered the northern verandah. Beautiful women, who shimmered with the radiance of swans on a lake, floated before my eyes in the dark interior. Each one held a fan in her hand. As soon as they saw us, the fans stopped moving and they hurried to the door.

'Kochu! Who is this child?'

'Bala's child, Kamala. She's come for the summer holidays. She goes back to Calcutta on the twelfth of Mithunam.'

'Sit down, Kochu.'

'Kamala, sit down.'

A woman spread out a grass mat with an image of a tiger on it. None of the women of the house sat with us.

They arranged themselves in various places—on the cot, the stone ledges and the floor—smiling at us and waving their fans. Their white clothes and fans reminded me of white birds. Birds that flew close to heaven. All of them had long, wavy hair, bright eyes and red lips. They wore jewellery fashioned in traditional designs. They smiled at me over and over again.

'She's not as fair as Bala, is she?'

'But she's not as dark as Madhavan Nair!'

'Lovely hair! What oil do you use for the child, Kochu?'

'Oil extracted directly from scraped coconut. I make enough and send it to Calcutta every year. They'll never be able to make it there.'

'The child is lucky to have a grandmother like you!'

'She's a lucky child. There's no doubt about that.'

'Is Amma Thampuran asleep?'

'No. She'll be here soon.'

When she appeared, the woman who had the title of Amma Thampuran did not wear a blouse. Her breasts were covered with a small cloth. She was plump and fair and had hair that was growing grey. Staring at me, she asked Ammamma, 'Isn't this Bala's child?'

'Yes.'

'Isn't her name Kamalam?

'We call her Kamala.'

'Let the child speak. Why are you answering all my questions, Kochu? Doesn't the child speak Malayalam?'

'Oh yes, she does. They speak Malayalam at home.'

'I suppose it's other languages she hears in Calcutta—English, Bengali and so on.'

'Yes.'

'Does she go to school?'

'Yes.'

'Which one?'

'St Cecilia's European School.'

'Why does Madhavan Nair send the child to a European school?'

'That's what he wanted.'

'Can't the child stay here? She'd be able to drink tender coconut water whenever she likes, eat mangoes and learn Malayalam from Nambidi Master. And she'd be a companion to you, Kochu. What do you say, Kamalam— why don't you decide not to return to Calcutta?'

I was really impressed by Amma Thampuran's intelligence. I was frightened of Achan, my father—more frightened than I was of Ammaman, my mother's uncle. Father had great expectations of his children. I could never rise up to them. An inferiority complex stung me whenever I was in Achan's presence, though in my grand-uncle's eyes, I was always a clever child.

While we were going back from the kovilakam, Ammamma told me that we had no right to touch any of the people who lived there and that they belonged to a caste different from ours.

'What will happen if I touch Amma Thampuran?' I asked.

'She'll have to take a dip in the pond. We are Nairs, remember. If Nairs touch them, they will be polluted.'

Ammamma explained the differences between castes. The Namboodiris were of the highest caste; then came the Thampurans. Below them were the Nairs, then the Thiyas, the Vettuvas, the Pulayas, the Parayas and the Nayadis. The poor Nayadi could only stand at the other end of a paddy field from where he could call out, 'Valia Thampuratti of Nalapat!' They were like the birds that sat on the highest branches of trees and cried in sing-song voices. I longed to go up and talk to them. But the Thiya woman who took them rice in a winnowing tray would never consent to take me along.

'You'll scream in fear if you see a Nayadi, Cheria Thampuratti. He looks like a kuthichudiyan. Haven't you seen our kuthichudiyan, the bird that sits on the kanhira tree in the snake shrine and hoots? The Nayadi looks like that. I'll never, never take you to see a Nayadi. No, I won't!'

One day, while I was having my kanji, Ammamma served me pappadams and I said, using the term of respect I had heard Valli use so often to her, 'Adiyan doesn't want pappadams.'

Ammamma was very amused. 'Why do you speak of yourself as "adiyan", Kamala? Can't you say "I"?'

'But that's what Valli says.'

'Valli's a Thiya by caste. You're not a Thiya.'

'Then what caste do I belong to?'

'If you haven't realized what caste you are by now, Kamala, you'll never understand even if I explain to you.'

It is now that I understand the truth of what Ammamma said.

❖

It was someone's birthday at Ambazhathel—I'm not sure whose—the day there was a cyclone. Ettan, my elder brother, and I were invited to the feast there that day. Malathikutty took us to the serpent shrine before lunch. We watched Meenakshi Edathi setting out turmeric, milk and bananas for the snakes.

Meenakshi Edathi was a distant relative of the Ambazhathel family. Being poor, she was dependent on their generosity. She was dark-skinned and middle aged. She spent her time rushing around the house and compound, never stopping to rest, her face perpetually wearing an expression that asked for forgiveness. She had only certain trivial duties to perform, like welcoming the oracle with an offering of paddy when he came in a procession, lighting all the lamps at dusk, churning the curd and taking out the butter for the children, and drawing designs with rice batter on the door on the day of the Nira festival. There were innumerable servants to carry out all the other tasks. However, the family could not have existed happily for a single day without Meenakshi Edathi. She was the only one who knew how much paddy should be boiled each time to make enough rice for the household or how many mundus had been given to the washerman or when to give the children a purgative.

'Why isn't the snake coming?' I asked.

'Snakes never come out when human beings are watching, child. The black Krishnasarpam will glide out as soon as we go away,' said Meenakshi Edathi.

I began to feel sleepy after lunch. Malathikutty came back with us to Nalapat. Barely an hour after we got home, we heard the sound of the gale.

The wind tore through the coconut palms in the southern compound with a frightening roar. The dry leaves that had collected around the pond swirled upwards belligerently. Branches shook. The seat of the swing that hung from the ilanji tree fell down.

'I wonder whether it's a cyclone . . . The sound of it scares me,' said Ammamma. She asked all of us to sit down in the middle room upstairs and gave us metal dice to play with. Since the light had grown dim, she lit a brass lamp as well.

Muthassi called out from the thekkini, the southern room, downstairs, 'Have you closed all the small windows, Kochu?'

'I'll close them, Amme; I'll close all of them,' answered Ammamma. We suddenly heard the sound of the rain from the south-west, like the roar of a vast crowd of people. Using all her force, Ammamma slammed the windows shut. Raindrops glimmered on her face.

'It's not even four, but it's pitch dark outside,' said Ammamma.

'I want to see Kutti Oppu,' said Malathikutty.

'She'll come by dusk,' said Ammamma.

'I want to go to Ambazhathel now, this minute,' said Malathikutty.

'I'll send you to Ambazhathel as soon as the storm stops.' Ammamma tried to comfort her, but Malathikutty began to sob loudly. That was when we heard a coconut palm crashing down.

'Kochu, what was that? Will the house collapse?' That was Muthassi.

'Don't worry. It was a coconut palm falling. We'll go and have a look at it once the rain stops. Let's say our prayers and sit here quietly,' said Ammamma.

All of us took shelter in the southern room downstairs as Ammaman's mother instructed us to do. She said this room had the strongest ceiling. The thekkini was flooded and the water that had collected in the sunken courtyard of the nalukettu, the central hall with four wooden pillars, began to overflow. Ammaman and all of us children sat on the bed. Ammamma and the grandmothers sat on the rolled-up mattresses stacked on the floor. And the servant woman took refuge in the makeshift toilet adjacent to the room.

Ammayi arrived, drenched to the skin, unmindful of the thunder and lightning and driving rain.

'How can you be so foolish, Bala? What if you fall ill of a fever?' asked Ammaman.

Ammayi laughed.

'Here's Kutti Oppu,' exclaimed Malathikutty joyfully. Ammayi hugged her.

Cheriamma suggested that we chant aksharaslokams to forget our fear: each one of us would have to recite a verse and the next person would follow with a verse that began with the first letter of the third line of the quatrain that had just been chanted. No one volunteered, though. So Cheriamma recited from Vallathol's *Imprisoned Aniruddhan*.

Ammamma said, 'I can't remember a single couplet.'

'I hope the house doesn't collapse,' murmured Muthassi.

As soon as Ammaman and Ammayi went upstairs, the servant woman started to wail loudly. She kept hitting her head with her hands while she wailed.

'What madness is this? Do you want to break open your head?' asked Ammamma.

'What if I never see my folks again . . . My Guruvayoorappa! I'll never see them again!'

'You can go home tomorrow morning, as soon as the rain stops. All right?' said Muthassi.

'This rain will never stop. It's a whirlwind, isn't it? We'll all die,' sobbed the woman.

'Is she crazy?' asked Muthassi. We heard trees crashing to the ground. And a dog whining in the western yard.

'Aiyo, Sankara! What if the cowshed crumbles? Bring the cows in and tie them up in the washing area outside the kitchen,' said Ammamma.

'The cowshed won't fall down, Valiamma. Its beams are quite strong,' said Sankaran Nair, who had gone to check things out.

'Then let the cows stay there.'

'There's knee-deep water in the yard now,' said Sankaran.

'We want to swim,' I cried.

'You can swim in the courtyard of the nalukettu,' said Ettan.

I put my hand into the water in the courtyard. 'It's ice-cold,' I grumbled.

'Don't play in the water, children,' Ammamma called out loudly. We climbed back on the bed. Someone seemed to be knocking on the door on the southern side. Sankaran opened it. A dog stood on the verandah, dripping wet—Thumbi, the black-and-white pet dog from Ambazhathel.

'Look, here's Thumbi. He's drenched. Poor thing, he must have come out with Balamani Amma,' said Sankaran.

We looked at Thumbi and he looked at us. He was shivering in the cold. Sankaran spread a gunny bag on the verandah. 'Lie down on this. In a storm like this, how can we make a difference between a man and a dog? Go to sleep, Thumbi.' Thumbi lay down on the gunny bag and looked contentedly at me and my brother.

We spent the whole night in the southern room. By the time we woke up, the rain had stopped.

It was the sound of a pleading voice saying 'Please open the gate' that actually woke me. A young man stood smiling in the waist-high water at the gate.

'I'm from Vadekkara. Is everyone here all right?'

'Yes,' said Ammamma. 'We've had no casualties. How did you come, Balan?'

'I started out at daybreak and waded through the water.'

'That's really smart!'

'The number of huts and trees that have collapsed! Fowls lying dead everywhere, dead goats floating in the water—what a sight!'

'Come in, Balan, and change your mundu.'

'Have they sent us anything from Vadekkara? Murukkus or dates?' I asked.

'No, child. I've come empty-handed,' said Balan, displaying his buck teeth.

'What a time to ask for murukkus and dates!' muttered Ammaman's mother. I hung my head, ashamed.

❖

Kunhan Nambisan was a short, phlegmatic man. He had the crumpled look of a banana that, instead of being steamed, had been cut and cooked in water. Somehow, he made me uneasy. His appearance was not pleasing in the least. You couldn't even tell whether his skin was fair or dark, or between the two. And he had patches all over his body. As for his voice, it was neither a man's nor a woman's; it sounded like that of a wounded owl, or a sparrow that had caught a cold. His speech was plentifully punctuated by grunts. Instead of saying yes or no, he would express his feelings in rhythmic, forceful grunts.

The karanavan of the Ambazhathel family, Keshavadasa Menon, was very fond of Nambisan's company and liked to see him at least twice a week. He realized no one had Nambisan's ability and patience to listen to everything he said and grunt appreciatively. No matter how often his salaried employees said 'Yes, Master' to him, Keshavettan did not feel gratified. Although the manager called Mannankandan used to praise him in all the ways he knew, Keshavettan was not sure his eulogies were sincere.

Since Kunhan Nambisan belonged to a high caste, his poverty did not prevent him from leading a pleasant social life. He was respected not only by the Ambazhathel taravad, or extended family, but also by the Thendiyath and Palasserry families and at the Eliyangode kovilakam. Punnayoorkulam had no listener as perfect as Nambisan. The patience to listen endlessly, the capacity to grunt approval whenever needed, the knack to fall asleep while people were being slandered, pretending he had heard nothing: who else had all these qualities?

No one ever spoke ill of Nambisan. They only found fault with his wife, Nangeli Brahmaniyamma. She had worn rowkas even when she was very young. Those were the days when society considered young women who wore rowkas too fashionable. Later, when women began to cover their breasts, society still found it hard to abandon its disapproval of Brahmaniyamma. She was a woman who had no beauty at all; even her voice was ugly.

When she stood before the inner shrine in the temple and sang a song of praise to God in her rough voice, the villagers would laugh softly among themselves. Her neighbours spread a rumour that she often scolded her husband, probably because she sounded angry even when she spoke normally. As she grew older, Brahmaniyamma began to talk to herself. I once heard her mutter, as she walked along the edge of the field, stamping on the punna flowers, 'How can one not slap an impudent child?'

Assuming that it was me she meant, I ran away. After that, I always hid when I saw her.

She knew everything about the fasts observed on occasions like Ekadashi and Shashti and often discussed these matters with the grandmothers at Nalapat. It was she who convinced Muthassi that the best food to have on Ekadashi day was gruel made from chaama, our Kerala millet. 'If you have wheat kanji twice a day, your stomach will begin to hurt,' she said.

'Yes, wheat generates heat, doesn't it?'

'Of course it does! Terrible heat! It's not good for the body at all.'

'But Punjabis and others eat chapattis made of wheat. They're not unhealthy, are they?'

Muthassi's question did not please Brahmaniyamma.

'Who's seen Punjabis anyway? How do we know whether they're healthy or not?'

'That's true; we've not seen any Punjabis.'

'Then how can you be sure, Ammukutty Amma, that they're healthy?'

Brahmaniyamma laughed, showing her worn teeth, stained with red. Muthassi shook her head, overcome.

'And doesn't chaama generate heat?' asked Ammamma.

'No, it's cool, like sago and arrowroot. If you don't believe me, ask our Kunhunni Nambisan.'

'I don't have to ask anyone, Brahmaniyamma. I believe you.'

'You must grind some coconut chutney to go with the chaama kanji. And have it with salted mango. Delicious. And you won't feel weak from the fast.'

'I'll never fast again on Ekadashi,' said the servant woman. 'I fasted last month and when I went to the temple in the evening, my legs gave way just as I began to circumambulate the shrine. Kalikutty, who works at Thendiyath, was with me. She was really frightened. I sat down right there—it was so painful. Cramps went up my legs. I couldn't get up until Kalikutty massaged my legs. Everyone who had come to worship crowded round me. The men kept staring at my legs. I nearly died, Brahmaniyamma. The Namboodiri said, don't fast on Ekadashi any more; you're not old enough for such things . . .'

'The Namboodiri is right. You're not old enough to fast on Ekadashi, Lakshmi.'

'There's no specific age for Ekadashi fasts,' proclaimed Brahmaniyamma. 'I don't remember a time when I didn't observe a fast on this day. If you're a Hindu, you have to fast on Ekadashi regardless of whether you're a man or a woman. How can you live a good life unless you please Sri Parameswaran?'

Everyone admitted that Brahmaniyamma was right.

❖

When it was not raining, carpenter Kunju worked under the mango tree in the northern yard. Or rather, he presided over the work done there. Other activities like the boiling of paddy and the drying of vegetable wafers on mats also took place under the mango tree. It was a vantage point: anyone who sat there could talk to the cook in the kitchen or the women in the pounding shed or people walking through the fields. It was the nerve centre of our world. Seated there chewing betel leaves and tobacco, Kunju would make little stools, grandmother-dolls, flat and rounded rulers and other wooden articles. All the dolls bore a resemblance to Valli: hair knotted above the head, pendulous breasts, no clothes except a short mundu.

One day I asked Kunju, 'Can't you make me a prettier doll?'

'Aren't the dolls that Kunju makes pretty?' he asked.

'They are, but . . .'

'A head and breasts: that's what women must have. They don't need anything else.'

I nodded. Kunju picked up a doll and went on, 'Doesn't this one have a head?'

'Yes.'

'Doesn't it have breasts?'

'Yes.'

'What more do you want?'

'Nothing. But I don't want this doll. You can take it home, Kunju.'

I ran up to Muthassi and climbed on to her lap. Ammamma was reading the *Ramayanam*.

'What's the matter, Kamala? Why are you breathing so hard?'

'Aren't there any other carpenters besides Kunju?'

'Why are you angry with Kunju, Kamala?'

'I don't want his dolls. All of them look like Valli. Why don't you send for another carpenter?'

'Who else will come and work here all day? They've all got other things to do.'

Kunju would lay his leaf on the ground and eat there. The cook would serve him two big ladles of rice. Kunju would make balls the size of a bitter lemon, dip one side of it in sambhar and eat greedily. Now and then he would bite into a roasted chilli. I would sit on the verandah and watch him eat. His eyes would fill and overflow as he ate.

'Do you like sambhar, Kunju?' I asked him.

'The sambhar here is not hot or sour enough for me. I can't eat food that is not pungent and sour.'

'Can you eat a hundred ground chillies, Kunju?'

'Why a hundred, I can eat a thousand! I've been used to it from childhood. The astrologer Pannikkar told me I have a demoniac nature, I'm an asuragana . . . and my birth-star is Triketta. Asuras like their food to be spicy. They drink toddy and arrack and eat meat and fish.'

Kunju's well-built figure was coppery in colour. And his face was bright red. While he boiled paddy, he would be enveloped from time to time in a haze of blue smoke. I would imagine then that he was a genie who had come out of a pot.

Kunju used to make various kinds of flat and rounded rulers for my elder brother. Ettan used to put them away safely in his study in the padippura, the gatehouse.

Kandaran, the master carpenter, built our padippura. When he arrived at Nalapat, a dark-skinned man with a wrinkled body, with a tuft knotted over his head and a tooth curved like a tiger claw, Ammaman himself went out to receive him.

'No one but you will be able to carry out this task,' said Ammaman. Kandaran smiled and his curved tooth trembled slightly.

'My eyesight is growing weak. I don't go out to work now,' he said.

Kunju knew Kandaran had come and gone. But he did not get up from where he was seated, under the mango tree, or go out to welcome him.

'Doesn't Kandaran make dolls?' I asked Ammamma.

'Don't you ask him to make you a doll now,' warned Ammamma.

'They send for all kinds of people to take measurements and all that. But when they really want something done, there'll only be Kunju to do it,' proclaimed Kunju. The women who were seated in the cowshed and the verandah laughed.

'It's true,' one of them agreed. 'Ultimately, Kunju's the only one who is really useful.'

❖

The Ambazhathel family, who were our neighbours and relatives, had a cook whom everyone knew: Kunju Nair. He was six feet tall and belonged to Edappal. Neither the kitchen nor the outhouse at Ambazhathel had high doors, which is probably why Kunju Nair learned to stoop while he walked. His mouth was always full of a reddish mixture of betel leaves and tobacco. He would come out of the kitchen from time to time, like a fish surfacing for fresh air, stand on the verandah holding on to the rafter, bend forward and spit forcefully. No one ever dared contradict Kunju Nair's pronouncements. He had his own opinion about everything that happened in the world.

Ambazhathel was a wealthy joint family. In those days, no one wanted to divide the family wealth and give each member an individual share.

Everyone appreciated the dishes Kunju Nair made. After his death, none of the cooks who succeeded him achieved his standards. People therefore lost interest in food, and apparently this was the most important provocation for dividing the wealth of the taravad later. It was the children of the family who told me these secrets.

The Ambazhathel house was beautiful. On the eastern side was a garden in which grew jamoon trees, many varieties of hibiscus and a mandaram tree. A mango tree cast its shade over the eastern yard. There were three pillars in the wide front verandah and cement ledges to sit on. Keshavadasa Menon used to recline on a cane bed there, with karyasthan Mannankandan, the manager of his property, seated on a platform next to him. Keshavadasa Menon was adept at solving the crossword puzzles in the weekly magazine. Whenever he was not sure of a word, he would say, 'I can't think of the right word, Mannankanda . . .'

'Think of Guruvayoorappan; imagine he's with you. Then the word you want will most certainly come to you.'

We once had a cook named Chappan Nair at Nalapat. He was a simple villager. Unlike the Chappan Nair at Punnayoorkulam, who was a military man, our Chappan Nair didn't speak English or Hindi. But no one who had tasted his ash-gourd sambhar could ever forget it. This must have been why the Ambazhathel children used to come over for lunch to Nalapat on most days. Every Thursday, they had dry roasted mutton at Ambazhathel. The Nalapat folk were vegetarians and never used onions or garlic in their cooking. Which was why I disliked the peculiar flavour of the food I first ate at Ambazhathel.

The Nalapat women did not usually eat in other people's houses. Nor would they eat in front of strangers. Later, with the advent of schools, colleges and new fashions, they had to change their way of living.

Once, when I came back from Ambazhathel, Ammamma asked me, 'Were there onions in all the vegetable curries there?'

Actually, all I had eaten there was rice and a curry made of roasted, pounded green gram. They had not served all the festive dishes, kalan and olan and erisserry, that Ammamma had presumed they would. I had spent five or six nights at Ambazhathel at the insistence of my friend who was part of the family. As a child, I did not ever dream that I would go to Ambazhathel one day as a bride.

Chappan Nair of Nalapat was a great bhaktha, a devotee. In the daytime, his forehead would be smeared with sandal paste and after dusk, with vibhuti. He was paid a salary of five rupees a month. He would ask Ammamma for small amounts from it the very first week of the month and gradually completely run through the sum. Ammamma would take out from her letter box the eight annas or thereabouts that remained on the first of the month and give it to him. Once a month, he put on a striped shirt and paid a visit to his village. He usually spent a night there. He always took along a paper packet of neyyappams and jaggery. 'They must be for his wife,' the servant woman would say. 'After all, he visits her only once a month. He can't go empty-handed. Poor man, he's so simple and good.'

Around this time, Lakshmi, who worked at Thendiyath, ate some raw cow dung. And not just a small amount. She ate a whole plateful. Unnimaya, who swept our yard, brought us the news. The boys at Thendiyath had said they would give her a nose ring if she ate a heap of cow dung and Lakshmi had collected the cow dung at once and begun to eat it! When she had finished, they said, 'We didn't realize you're such a filthy creature. You can't work here any more.'

'The wretch! She got the punishment she deserved. Brainless creature!'

However, Lakshmi was back at her work a week later. She was no longer called Lakshmi though. The village knew her now as Pacchha-chanakam-theeni or Eater of Raw Cow Dung and she was no longer allowed to enter people's kitchens. All she could do was sweep the floor and smear it with cow dung.

One of our neighbours went mad around this time. He let his beard and hair grow long, gave up bathing and sleeping and sat on the sand in the yard, staring at the sun. One day, when Amma's uncle and his friend Marathattil Sankaran Nair passed that way, he got up and salaamed.

'Gandhi jai! Kasturibai jai!' he cried loudly. Ammaman repeated this to us and we laughed endlessly.

'He's quite crazy. Did he think Ammaman was Kasturba? Or Sankaran Nair?' I asked Ammamma, but she did not give me an answer.

❖

When I was a child, we did not have television or the cinema in our village. Maybe that was why everyone tried to make the entertainment of guests a real art. The hosts would serve the most delicious food and drink to persuade the guests to prolong their stay.

Guests who came to Nalapat liked to stay there for at least a week. Most of the time, they relaxed in the front verandah, paying no heed to the passage of time as they savoured Ammaman's conversational skills. Many of them were well-known people. Advocates, literary figures, diplomats, expert physicians, astrologers: they were all Ammaman's friends.

His closest friend was most certainly Sri Kuttikrishna Marar, who used to visit Nalapat at least twice a year. Each time he came, he stayed two weeks. Someone hinted in an article published after Ammaman's death that he had not lent Marar money when he needed it. This must have been why Marar did not visit Nalapat during the last few years of Ammaman's life.

Ammaman lived like a king, but he did not have much money. It was not easy to sell books. Marar's request for money must have distressed Ammaman deeply. He probably did not want to declare his poverty openly. Whatever it was, the two close friends evidently parted company because of a misunderstanding. I used to lie on Ammamma's lap in the thekkini trying to listen while Marar conversed with Ammaman. Marar had a feeble voice; so I could never follow what he said. Ammaman's voice was firm and, of course, familiar to me.

When I told Ammaman of my desire to learn Malayalam, he gave me Marar's *Malayalashailee,* a book of grammar. It was from reading this book that I acquired mastery of the language.

Marar was very shy. He would speak to no one except Ammaman. He used to take a walk along the edge of the snake shrine and through the western compound. The women would stand at the windows and look at him through the bars when he went to the privy situated far away from the house. Indeed, they looked at all the visitors through the window bars. It was easy to catch a glimpse of those who came to eat with Ammaman in the thekkini: they could be seen through the slats of the vadikkini window. Muthassi and Ammamma never stared at anyone for long. None of the guests was good-looking enough to capture attention.

I remember that the guest who ate the most was Chelanattu Achutha Menon. There was a Sankaran Nair who used to turn up at Nalapat occasionally, a man who talked angrily about agriculture and the landlord–tenant relationship all the time. Everyone was afraid of him. An advocate called Govinda Menon used to come for three-day visits. There was an astrologer, Shoolapani Variar, who was very dear to Ammaman. Ammaman used to get his horoscope and those of his family scrutinized by Variar over and over again. I don't know whether he did so because he believed in astrology or because he found it amusing. Maybe Ammaman considered all branches of knowledge sources of amusement. He dabbled in all of them, but never plunged deeply into any.

I saw Ammaman grieve only once. When his mother's body was wrapped up and carried by her relatives to the southern yard to be cremated, Ammaman was lying in the southern room, his body full of diabetic carbuncles. Leaning back in bed, he suddenly broke down and began to weep. His sobs astonished me. I would never have believed that the Ammaman who always comforted us when we cried, saying, 'Now, now, don't cry,' could himself weep. He never used to speak to his mother. He would come to the door of the thekkini and say something loudly as if he was addressing all the women inside—that was all. If he ever asked a question, it was Ammamma who answered, as the sole representative of the women of the house.

The grandmothers spent their days in prayer. They chanted prayers continually, starting with *Narayana, Rama Rama, Namah Shivaya*. Ammaman's mother and Ammamma's mother, our Muthassi, wore chains of tulasi beads set in gold. And rings of gold, silver, copper and steel on their fingers.

Once, Vazhenkunnam Namboodiri came to stay with Ammaman at Nalapat for a few days. Ammaman told us that he was an expert in magic. Surrendering to our insistent demands, Vazhenkunnam conducted a performance on our patio. I remember him taking off our rings, burying them here and there and later plucking them from the air. And then, at the end of the show, I found Devaki lying on the floor in the vadikkini, sweating profusely.

'What happened, Devaki?' I asked her.

'I felt someone tug at my chain and thrust a hand into my blouse. I couldn't bear it, child. My legs gave way.'

'Who would thrust a hand into your blouse, Devaki?'

'That Namboodiri, the magician. Who else?'

'But he was standing so far away from you. He wouldn't even have seen you, Devaki.'

'He saw me all right. He was staring at me while he stood far away, performing magic. He looked as if he wanted to drink my blood!'

'You're just imagining things, Devaki,' said Muthassi. 'If you talk ill of people like him, God will punish you.'

'Oh yes! People can stare at me and do whatever they like to me! I don't have anyone to speak for me, do I?' lamented Devaki.

'Why are you so angry with the Namboodiri, Amral?' asked Unnimaya.

'There's no man you're not angry with, is there, Devaki?' I asked.

'You know what's in my heart, child,' murmured Devaki. She stood up and gave Sankaran, who was leaning against a pillar, a stern look. 'If you trust men, they'll betray you, child. They'll sweet-talk you in the beginning and then betray you.'

'Have men betrayed *you*, Devaki?' I asked.

'No one can, child. No great man can come along and take me for a ride. Let them keep their desires to themselves!'

In response to Devaki's loud rants, Sankaran gathered the phlegm in his throat, spat noisily into the yard and disappeared into the kitchen. Unnimaya, who was chopping jackfruit, lowered her head and shook so hard with silent laughter that a bit of the sticky exudation from the fruit stuck to the tip of her nose!

❖

One afternoon, as soon as Ammamma went upstairs after lunch to rest, Lakshmi the servant ran up and whispered in my ear, 'The korathi's come.'

'Who?'

'The korathi who reads palms. Haven't you seen a korathi, child? She's brought a parrot too. If you give her a coin, the parrot will pick up a card in its beak. Your destiny will be written on it, child.'

'Where's Korathi?'

'I've sat her down in the pounding shed. If Valiamma sees her, she won't allow her to read your palm.'

The korathi was seated on the ground in the pounding shed, nursing her baby. Her skin was the colour of milky coffee. Her forehead and chin were covered with dark green dots.

She smiled at me. Milk dribbled from the corner of the baby's mouth. It seemed to me then that the baby was smiling at me.

'Is your name Korathi?' I asked. My question displeased Lakshmi.

'Why are you asking her such foolish questions, child? Do korathis have names? They don't have pet names or family names or anything. They wander from house to house. They don't have a home or a village of their own.'

'Where do they sleep at night?'

'Under trees. Or in a cave on a mountain. Isn't that right, korathi?'

The korathi nodded, looked at me and smiled. Her mouth was full of crushed betel leaves, perhaps the reason why her lips were so red.

'Why do you have those dots on your forehead and chin?'

Lakshmi explained. 'They've been tattooed. Korathis and koravans, their menfolk, get themselves tattooed. The pattern is traced with a needle on the skin till it draws blood and the area is smeared with the juice of a leaf.'

The korathi had still not said a word. The torrent of words that streamed from Lakshmi's mouth began to get on my nerves. I didn't want her to answer the questions I was asking the korathi. I brushed off Lakshmi's hand and went close to the korathi.

'Move back, child,' screamed Lakshmi. 'Don't touch the korathi. Her body is covered with dirt.'

In spite of having been insulted, the korathi continued to smile. I saw my face reflected in her eyes. The mixed odour of tobacco and newly turned earth rose from her.

'Stand back, child, or I'll call Valiamma this minute. If you touch the korathi, you'll have to take a bath. Don't you know they wander all over the place?'

'Where's your house, korathi?' I asked. Still she wouldn't speak. It was as if she thought her smile was an answer to all my questions.

'Don't you know korathis don't have homes? Didn't I tell you that, child? You don't believe me, do you?'

'Go away. Go to sleep, Lakshmi,' I said.

'Oh yes. And suppose the korathi grabs the chance to run away with you?'

The korathi shook her head. Her eyes gleamed.

'You won't run away with me, will you, korathi?' I asked.

'No,' she said.

'The child will give you a couple of coins. Will you read her palm and mine?' said Lakshmi. 'Open the cage and let the parrot out. Let it pick a card.'

It was only then that I noticed the parrot. The cage was covered with a red cloth. The korathi took off the cloth, picked up the cage and brought it close to my face.

'Tathamma's not well. She won't pick a card today.'

'If the parrot doesn't pick a card, you won't get any money,' said Lakshmi.

The korathi's face became cheerless.

'Tathamma's not well at all. She hasn't eaten a thing today.'

I saw the little dish inside the cage. It was full of grain.

'Shall we give it some milk?' I asked.

'Tathamma won't drink anything. Tathamma's ill.'

'What's wrong with it?'

'Diarrhoea. It shits all day and all night. Because of the evil eye.'

'Will it die?' I asked.

'I don't know, Amma,' she said.

'How old is it?' I asked.

'It's 300 years old, Amma,' she said.

'Three hundred? Don't tell such whopping lies, korathi,' said Lakshmi.

'It's not a lie, Amma. It's the truth. It's my father's mother's parrot. And she got it from her father.'

'What's its name?'

'Chivakami.'

'So it's a she-parrot, then?'

'Yes, it is.'

The korathi took the parrot out and kissed the top of its head. The baby, which had been asleep on her lap, woke up and began to cry.

'Can I touch the parrot?' I asked.

'It'll fly away from the child's hand. Don't give it to her,' said Lakshmi.

'Tathamma can't fly. She's ill,' said the korathi.

I stroked it. To my astonishment, I discovered a vein throbbing in its throat. The parrot spread its wings once, then shrank into my palm with an air of defeat. I blew away the dust and chaff off its wings.

'Shall I put it on the ground?'

'Tathamma can't fly,' said the korathi.

The parrot hobbled towards the pounding stone. It picked up a grain of paddy lying near it. Its left foot was lame.

'What's happened to its foot?' asked Lakshmi.

'The cat grabbed it through the bars of the cage. If you give me money, Amma, I can read your palm.'

I gave her an anna.

'*Never will you drink/Kanji served with disrespect,*' she sang, looking at my left palm. Then she went out and spat the betel leaves on to the sand.

'Can you tell me when I'll get married?' Lakshmi asked, holding out her square, calloused hand and closing her eyes as if she were meditating. I couldn't help laughing. 'Why are you laughing, child? Don't poor people get married as well?'

The korathi cleared her throat. She stared at Lakshmi's palm for a long time.

'You don't have a marriage line, Amma,' she said.

'You mean I'll never get married as long as I live?'

'No. But the lines show that you'll have children. Two boys and three girls.'

'Oh God! Will I be betrayed then? Will that low-born rascal betray me?'

Lakshmi began to cry loudly. The korathi fastened the ends of her rowka tightly. She threw the bundle with the baby over her shoulder, picked up the parrot's cage and hurried away towards the fence.

'My coin's gone too!' wailed Lakshmi.

'It's not yours, Lakshmi. I gave her the anna, didn't I?'

'Oh, the child's lost her money! These wretched korathis shouldn't be allowed into the house. If Valiamma gets to know, it's me she'll scold.'

'But the korathi came because you called her in, Lakshmi.'

'Indeed! I never bring these creatures in. Who asked her to come in?' She lowered her voice. 'Maybe it was Sankaran Nair.'

❖

There was no doubt at all that Ezhikottil Karthyayani Teacher was the Empress of Culture in the Punnayoorkulam of that period, the period when the baby Vasu, who would later be known as M.T. Vasudevan Nair, was being suckled at his mother's breast.

The Teacher-Empress taught the third standard at school.

Karthyayani Teacher also taught the girls the traditional group dances: Kaikkottikkali, where they clapped and danced to the rhythm of their song, and Kolattam, where they danced holding wooden sticks in their hands.

Standing in the northern yard of the Rama Varma Raja Elementary School with the children around her, she sang about the games the infant Krishna played in a strange mixture of Malayalam and Tamil. The children sang after her in sweet, high voices, but they did not understand the meaning of the song.

Nevertheless, the whole school was enraptured by her singing. The headmaster, Chami Iyer, who taught mathematics; Elachar Teacher, who taught English; Thachu Master, who taught geography; Sukumaran Master, who taught history; Nambidi Master, who taught Malayalam; and Peter Master, who taught weaving: all of them suddenly fell silent. They were as puzzled as the children by the Tamil words.

Karthyayani Teacher was always surrounded by flatterers. Most of them were girls who displayed great enthusiasm to discuss other people's vagaries. It was an era when righteous anger was upheld as a virtue. Teacher prided herself on being the fountainhead of justice.

She generally wore saris with a dotted design. She had a certain unsophisticated charm, with her oiled curly hair loosely bound by a cord, her eyes touched with kajal, a pink sindooram mark on her forehead and an occasional smile that revealed teeth stained red with betel. She had unbounded arrogance.

It was Teacher's creative imagination that usually gave shape to the anniversary celebrations at school. She was very enthusiastic about choreographing dances for songs. And these performances generally won great applause. One year, during the anniversary function, a girl in a red skirt, with talcum powder smeared all over her face, opened the evening's programme with a number Teacher had taught her. She danced to the accompaniment of a song, greeting the respected president and other invitees. Putting her head out anxiously from behind the curtain every now and then, Teacher supervised the dance.

I longed to greet an audience like that one day, with talcum smeared all over my face. I was sure that if Teacher wanted to she could transform me into an artist.

When I described the performance to Ammaman, he said, 'Recite that poem to me again; I want to hear it.'

I sang the verse which was a mixture of Malayalam and Tamil.

'Che, che!' said Ammaman. 'What a silly song! I'm going to tell Chami Iyer not to allow the children to sing such foolish verses.'

'Ayyo,' I said, 'Teacher will slap me.'

'Slap you? That Ezhikottil Karthyayani slap my Aami? Just let me see her do that!'

After this incident, I used to hide in the thekkini whenever Karthyayani Teacher walked past our house with her retinue. I was terrified that Ammaman would call her in and talk to her about her song and she would become my enemy. But Ammaman never called her in, not once. He told the headmaster that it was not right to teach children to sing Malayalam songs that had Tamil words.

'They should either be completely in Tamil or in pure Malayalam. The two languages shouldn't be mixed.'

It was from the day Ammaman said this that the children of Punnayoorkulam began to sing verses composed by Vallathol, Kumaran Asan and Changampuzha, the great poets of Kerala. It was as though a cultural revolution had taken place in the village.

Around this time the, Om Parabrahmodaya theatre troupe staged its play 'The Mendicant' in Punnayoorkulam. A temporary stage was put up north of the school in an empty lot that belonged to the Ambazhathel family. Stalls appeared in the vicinity the day before the performance, displaying groundnuts, Mysore bondas, halva, bananas, coloured sherbets and other delicacies for sale. The very best seats cost a rupee. I sat with a fast-beating heart on one of them, between Amma and my elder brother, waiting for the curtain to rise.

First of all there was a song.

The Om Parabrahmodaya Dramatic Troupe. What a splendid name! I thought the name was a song in itself.

The curtain rose at the end of the invocatory song.

A bearded beggar appeared. His face was painted white and his cheeks bright red. With him was a young girl. The beggar looked at us and sang in a heart-rending voice.

'We are the most pitiful of beggars,
The most pitiful of beggars you can see.'

I began to sob.

'Stop it, Kamala. It's only a play. Don't start crying now.'

'We should never have brought Aami for this play,' said my elder brother. I wiped my tears with the hem of my frock.

Obviously encouraged by all this, the beggar began to relate the story of his life. He told us that his daughter had no one in the world except him. The girl stared unblinkingly at us. I noticed that the edge of her skirt was torn. But she had red lipstick on her lips and talcum powder on her face.

A small boy selling sesame balls sweetened with jaggery edged up to us. I longed to eat one of them.

'Che, che!' said Ammamma. 'Imagine wanting to eat things like that, Kamala! I'm really surprised at you! We'll make sesame balls at home tomorrow, all right?'

I nodded. Ammamma was more interested in looking around her and smiling at the spectators she recognized than in watching the play. She evinced much pleasure at seeing the Eliyangode princesses, Ammu Amma of Palisserry and Koliyath Lakshmikutty Amma and smiled radiantly at each of them.

'It's just like going for a wedding, isn't it, Kamale? You can meet everyone here.'

Actually, only my brother really watched the play. Most of the spectators kept talking to one another. Every now and then, a woman would get up, calling out, 'Appunni . . .' or 'Sushila . . .' or 'Mani . . .'

Karthyayani Teacher had a one-rupee seat.

There were people seated on the ground. Some of them were asleep, lying on the ground. When the music started, those who were asleep woke and scrambled up. When they turned their heads, I saw the glare of the petromax lamp reflected in their eyes. The petromax lamp hissed like a snake. A man in a white shirt got on to a stool from time to time and pumped the lamp.

'These lamps sometimes explode. Like a bomb,' said Thomas Master, a man with a mustache, giving everyone an innocent smile.

'That was what happened in Angamali. Forty-one people died,' Thomas Master continued his narration. His smile was dazzling. A woman who sat behind me got up.

'I'm going. I don't want to see the play. Imagine, all these people will die if this thing explodes!'

'Sit down, Ammini Edathi. Once you're born, you have to die. What's the point of being so frightened? You paid a rupee, didn't you, to see the play?'

The members of the drama troupe were standing right at the back, hushing the audience from time to time. They had to drive away all those who were loitering in the vicinity or climbing up mango trees to watch the play without buying tickets. They frequently had to grope around in the darkness, searching for these miscreants. I heard the sound of a slap and a rough voice say, 'I'll throw you in the well now!'

A sudden murmur arose from the spectators: 'CR is coming. CR.' I turned. Kallukattayil Kochunni Nair had arrived with his family, accompanied by servants carrying hurricane lanterns. He wore a striped shirt, a double mundu and had a long angavastram on his shoulder. He was well built and a smile hovered at the corner of his eyes.

'They've just begun. Shall we ask them to start again, Master?'

'No, no.'

A line of new chairs appeared. His sisters were with him, as was my friend Bhanu, the daughter of one of the sisters.

'They've all come,' said Ammamma. 'I was wondering why there was no one from there. Now they've come too. Kuttappa Menon is here, Lakshmikutty Amma and the children, everyone from Palisserry, Manian Menon, all the Kalathingal folk and Doctor Kumaran.'

Ammamma seemed really happy. As she paid no attention to the play, she did not have to grieve with the actors and actresses as I did.

When we were back at Nalapat, the cook said he had been to the play too.

'I climbed up the school wall. I could see very well from there.'

'Did you like the song the beggars sang, Sankara?'

'I don't remember any of the songs, child. That girl was very pretty.'

❖

There was a tall pala tree at the western boundary of the Nalapat compound. If you stood under it, you could see the washerwoman Lakshmikutty's unplastered house and even the fumes that rose from the clothes when she washed them in water mixed with ash. If you stared a little harder, you could see Bala, Lakshmikutty's daughter, sitting on the verandah playing kothankallu, tossing the stones up and catching them as they fell. Bala never evinced the slightest interest in helping her mother. All she wanted was to learn to sing. Whenever our blind Kuttappa Bhagavathar sang at Nalapat, Bala would come there to listen. She once bought a music book at the Guruvayoor temple. Lakshmikutty wanted to buy her some dates, glass bangles and coloured cotton cloth, but Bala was quite satisfied with her music book and did not want anything else.

Lakshmikutty went to the Guruvayoor temple on the first of every month and also on important festival days. Like Ammamma, she was a devotee of Krishna. But Ammamma never visited Guruvayoor on festival days. She could not bear the crowds.

'Was there a crowd on Ekadashi day?' she would ask Lakshmikutty.

'You should have seen—what a crowd! Not an inch of unoccupied space! I carried the child on my shoulder; otherwise she'd have been trampled to death!' said

Lakshmikutty. Her smile had the pristine whiteness of freshly starched clothes which had been dipped in blue.

Lakshmikutty used to take one of the servant women at Nalapat to keep her company when she went to Guruvayoor. Most times, it was Devaki, who would describe the day's events to me when she got back. Guruvayoor was six miles away from Nalapat. The Kallaimana pond was situated halfway. They would go down to it and have a wash before going on. If they were lucky, someone would offer them tender coconuts or buttermilk on the way. After worshipping at the temple they would have tea, dosa, vada and sweet sukhiyan at the Hotel de Krishna. They would do some shopping after that and buy innumerable bangles, clothes, murukkus, puffed rice and dates. Packing all these things into a gunny-cloth bag with a picture of Gandhiji on it, they would start back home.

'Soon after we passed Vailathur, my mother and Devaki Edathi squatted under a coconut palm to urinate,' said Bala.

Ammamma usually went to Guruvayoor by boat. We would all walk in procession to the river at dawn, with Mambulli Krishnan leading, waving a blazing palm-leaf torch. His wife, Valli, followed right behind him. I was next, perched on someone's shoulder. Ammamma followed with a servant carrying a hurricane lantern behind her. The dry chirp of crickets rose ceaselessly from the lemongrass and screw pine that lined the banks of the river. Now and then, a frog put out a pale leg and hopped forward.

Kelu, who rowed the boat, had badly lacerated lips. 'What's the matter with them?' I once asked Devaki.

'He has ulcers in his mouth,' she answered.

'Will I get ulcers too?' I asked.

Devaki didn't reply. Kelu kept smiling at me as he rowed. I sat on the middle seat, near Devaki. Ammamma unrolled a grass mat in the boat, spread a mundu over it and lay down. Once, Ammamma leaned over the boat and threw up in the water. Another time, she plucked a water lily and gave it to me. Devaki said she knew how to weave chains with stems of the water lily.

I remember bathing in the tank of the Bhagavathi temple as soon as we reached Guruvayoor. A stout devotee who stood leaning against a pillar watched us while we bathed. Every now and then, he pretended he was playing a flute.

'That's our Snake-Govindan,' said Devaki. 'He's crazy, but quite harmless. He doesn't give anyone any trouble. He thinks he's the god Unni Krishnan.'

Once we had worshipped in the temple and made our offerings, we'd walk to Achan's taravad. I would try to persuade Ammamma to go to the Hotel de Krishna. But she would firmly grip my hand and step on to the red path that led to the Mammiyoor temple.

Wild jasmine and four-o'-clock and shanku flowers grew in Vadekkara, Achan's taravad. There was an almond tree just beyond the gate.

As soon as we arrived, Achan's sister would welcome us with idlis and tea. After eating, I would leave the women and go to the porch. An old man affectionately known as Chemban would be waiting there to teach me drawing.

'If you learn how to draw elephants and hands, you've learned everything,' he would say. He once gave me a book full of pictures of elephants and hands. He also taught me how to carve chessmen out of banana stems.

Soon after my brother and I had learned to play chess, Ammamma said, 'Go and play upstairs; otherwise someone will cast an evil eye on you.' Ammamma thought of us as exceptionally intelligent children. Smiling to herself, she would listen attentively to us speaking to each other in

English. But the other children started to tease us for speaking in English. They would shout, 'Look, look, they're shitting English!' Afraid of this taunt, we abandoned the language.

Meanwhile we were uncertain when the Second World War would end and we would be able to return to Calcutta.

❖

On one occasion, when my father came down from Calcutta, he was angry to see how wild my hair had grown. He thought I looked absolutely unkempt.

'Send for Chathu tomorrow. We have to cut this child's hair.'

Ammamma's pale face grew paler when she heard what Achan said. But she did not dare oppose him in any way.

Achan went on, 'With an appearance like this, I'll never get her into a Calcutta school! Once her hair is cut short, I can get her in.'

I had been in Ammamma's care for about two years. A period during which she had drawn the deepest satisfaction from rubbing freshly made coconut oil into my hair every day, then washing out the oil with powdered green gram, drying my hair and combing it neatly.

Chathu presented himself the next morning. He enjoyed cutting Achan's hair because Achan would ask him about everything that had happened in Punnayoorkulam after he had left for Calcutta. In addition, he gave Chathu ten times the money others gave.

'Why are you going back to Calcutta? Everyone here says bombs are falling there.'

'No bombs have fallen yet. Let them fall if they want to. How can I hide in this village, fearing the war?' asked Achan, laughing.

'What guts!' murmured Chathu, shaking his head.

Achan was happy. He asked Chathu how much money he would need to open a haircutting saloon.

Chathu tucked the razor behind his ear and scratched his head.

'I don't know, Master. Chathu can't calculate things like that.'

'Think about it, Chathu. I'll be here until the fourth of next month. Tell me after you've really thought about it. I'll give you the money.'

Chathu's smile grew dazzling. He spat the reddish mixture in his mouth on to the roots of a coconut palm. He was so delighted that he waved his hands and shooed away the crows that were witnesses to this offer. 'Away with you, crows!' he cried as they pattered over the mat on which tamarind had been laid out to dry.

Chathu's movements were like those of a lifeless rag doll whose seams had come undone under the arms and thighs. I always thought he found it difficult to keep his long arms and legs under control.

Achan asked Chathu to cut my hair short. 'That's the fashion now in Calcutta for girls.'

Achan went on, 'Do you know how to do a bob? Her hair shouldn't touch her shoulders. Cut it to a length of two or three inches.'

Achan asked me to sit down on a chair and wrapped a bedsheet around me. Chathu moved his old, blackened scissors five or six times through the sand.

'To sharpen it,' he explained.

Ammamma's pale face, which had been at the window until then, disappeared.

'You know that sayib at Andithode? His wife is from our village. When she married the sayib, she cut her hair and became a madaama, a white woman. It was I who cut it for her. This Chathu knows how to bob women's hair, Master.'

Thick curls of hair kept falling to the ground around me.

'You know our women have a bit of hair on their legs. Madaamas don't have any. I believe they shave it off every day. Remember our Appunni from Perindiri, that jaundiced fellow? It was he who told me. He used to work in a sayib's house as a gardener. The madaama would never call him Appunni; she called him "kattnayar". Maybe she thought he was a Nair because of his complexion! You know he doesn't have a father. That's why he's so fair. But how was the madaama to know that? It wouldn't have worked if Appunni had told her that his mother wasn't a Nair. So Appunni never said a word. Whenever she needed him, she'd say, "Kattnayar, come, come." And "Ko, ko, kattnayar," when she wanted him to leave. He learned her language too, in the end. Imagine, our Appunni! He's got brains. Must be the offspring of some important person in Perindiri. Or some teacher's . . . who knows? Anyway, it was he who told me that madaamas shaved their legs every day. That's why their legs shine like that, you know. You must have seen a lot of them in Calcutta, Master . . .'

Achan burst out laughing.

Ammamma's face appeared again at the window of the thekkini.

Achan said he was satisfied with my new appearance. He called out to my mother, who was at work inside.

'Look, child. How does our Aami look now?'

Amma smiled but said nothing. Ammamma's eyes were red. She took me to the tank for a bath. She didn't say a word while she bathed me.

'Have I lost all my beauty?' I asked.

Ammamma did not answer.

❖

The first time the bangle seller who came to be known as Cherappan appeared in the eastern yard of Nalapat was after the feast on my seventh birthday. Everyone had gone upstairs for a nap.

The Chettys who went to Guruvayoor to sell bangles during the Ekadashi festival used to come by our place once a year with their wooden boxes on their way back home. Even if they had done a brisk trade, the boxes would still contain gilt bangles wrapped in red tissue paper, combs, glass bangles and pink silk ribbons.

But this unfamiliar bangle seller had only chipped glass bangles, a few plastic bangles and a greasy packet in his cardboard box.

'Who do you think you are, fellow, to break the fence and get in?' asked the cook, who was seated on the big wooden rice chest.

'It was broken. So I got in that way . . .'

'Do all the passers-by have to come in just because we've decided not to build a new fence this year?'

'I'll go away, Nair. I came in because I saw the child. My name is Cherappan. I'm from Chalisserry. If you want rubber bangles, child, I have some in my box.'

'Are you mad? Do you think our child can get only your rubber bangles to wear? Whose child do you think she is? I don't think you've ever heard of V.M. Nair! Which back-of-beyond village are you from? Is there anyone on the face of this earth who hasn't heard of V.M. Nair?'

'And how are you so sure, Nair, that I haven't heard of him?'

Cherappan sat down on the verandah and lit a beedi.

'Do you want a beedi, Nair?'

'I don't smoke beedis. I sometimes chew a bit of tobacco. Been chewing betel for two years now.'

'I knew that when I saw your mouth!' said the bangle seller.

The cook did not like his sass. He stood up and roared, 'Get up, fellow! Imagine sitting down on the verandah like this! The Nalapat verandah is not for Nasranis who've come from God-knows-where to sit on. Get out of here!'

'So, will you be polluted if I sit here then? Nasranis are not polluted, Nair. If they touch you it's like purificatory water being sprinkled over you. You know that dark-skinned oaf who does the puja in the Korangode temple? That Vadoor Namboodiri? It was he who told me that Nasranis are not polluted.'

'Maybe you're not polluted. But you stink. Don't sit near the child. If Valiamma wakes up and comes down, she'll scold you till you turn blind.'

Cherappan opened his packet and hastily stuffed a handful of rice in his mouth.

'It's rice mixed with coconut oil. And a mackerel, smeared with chilli powder and fried. My sister gave it to me.'

'What did you say? A mackerel? Bhagavathi, my goddess, if they hear about this inside, they'll throw me and the child out! They'll certainly have to perform a purificatory ceremony now!' The cook placed both his hands on his head, rolled his eyes and circumambulated the bangle seller. His voice rose, 'Get out now, will you? I must know, at once: will you go or not?'

'I'll go, you Nair. But let me sell some bangles first. I've not sold a thing today. I won't go back to my family without a couple of annas at least.'

'And who will buy your bangles here? There are only three grandmothers here. And then this child. Who do you think will answer for it if you put your worthless bangles on this child's hands?'

'Would you like some rubber bangles, child?' asked the bangle seller, smiling.

I nodded.

He held out bangles that reminded me of fish with stripes on their backs.

'How many do you want, child?'

'I want ten on each hand.'

'This Cherappan doesn't have so many bangles, little one. You can have six on each hand. All right? For just three annas.'

'I want four rubber bangles too,' said the servant woman.

'I don't have your size now. I'll bring some next month.'

'You should remember you'll never get bangles your size when you eat like a pig! Don't keep eating stale rice,' said the cook.

'Guruvayoorappa! There he goes, cursing me again. When I get up tomorrow, I won't be able to walk.'

'Why, does this Nair have a black tongue? Will his curses come true?'

The cook laughed loudly.

'Your sister must be the one with the black tongue!'

'Why blame my sister? What do you have against her?'

The cook laughed again. He groped on the ledge above the kitchen door, found some coins and gave them to Cherappan. 'Here, your three annas. You'd better go before Valiamma wakes up and comes down. She'll be furious. The whole verandah stinks—thanks to your sister and her fried fish!'

'It doesn't stink; you're just imagining it. I'm going, child.'

I used to buy bangles from Cherappan every summer holiday after that.

Cherappan came that way when I visited the village as a middle-aged woman in 1975. His curly hair had gone grey. His clothes were the same I remembered.

'It's Cherappan, isn't it?' I asked.

'Yes.'

'Do you have rubber bangles?'

'In your size, Amme?'

'Yes.'

'No. I only have small-sized bangles, for children.'

'Let me see.'

Nylon bangles, chipped glass ones, an oily packet . . .

'What's in the packet?'

'A handful of rice. Mixed with coconut oil. And a mackerel. Smeared with chilli powder and fried.'

'Did your sister fry it for you?'

'My sister? I don't have sisters. The only one I had died fifteen years ago. My younger daughter fried this fish. My Mary.'

'Do you remember coming here long ago, Cherappa? There was a child called Kamala here. She used to buy rubber bangles from you.'

'Ah . . . that child. I remember her. She went away to Calcutta. I never saw her after that. I heard she died. She was such an affectionate thing.'

'Who told you she died?'

'I heard, at Kottapadi . . . It seems she died in a hospital. My heart broke. She was my life. She'd call, Cherappa, Cherappa and come running behind me. She smiled all the time, that child. Poor thing, she died.'

❖

We children used to call my Ammayi's younger sister's eldest daughter Leela Oppu. She was slim and very tall, with skin the colour of sesame oil. Although they were thick, her lips were attractive. Tossing her shoulders, she would walk as if she didn't care what anyone thought of her. We tried to copy her gestures and mannerisms. She never deigned to play with us. She'd always brush us away, saying, 'Get lost, children!' with all the arrogance of a sixteen-year-old.

One day a love letter fell out of one of Leela Oppu's books. A man had written that he could not live even a day without his beloved Leela. Her uncles and aunts discussed the letter for a while and then sent for the heroine and held it out to her. Leela Oppu took it and burst out laughing.

'Whose letter is this?' asked Ammaman.

'Ammalu wrote it—one of my classmates.'

Soon after, the family had the blameless Leela Oppu married to a young man who worked in Andhra Pradesh.

Sarada Oppu, another sister of Ammayi's, brought Malathikutty and me silk jackets to wear for the wedding. They were pale blue, with flowers and creepers embroidered on them in coloured thread. I was wonderstruck at their beauty and brilliance. Never in all my life before or after that moment did I receive such a marvellous gift. Ammamma had written to Sarada Oppu to get it for me, having no other way of indulging my great desire to have one. Appeals of that kind only disgusted my father. He wanted his children to wear only inexpensive, unostentatious clothes. Indeed, the lifestyle he permitted us was our punishment for having been born his children.

The softness of the blue jacket caressed me. I wore a chain with a pendant that had a beautiful carving of Krishna lying on a banyan leaf and Malathikutty wore Ammayi's necklace set with precious stones. Leela Oppu was a lovely bride in her yellow silk sari, with long strands of flowers in her hair. After her wedding, I began to put up my hair and learned to weave the jasmine buds that grew near the well into long strands.

All of us respected Sarada Oppu. She lived in Coimbatore with her engineer husband, Kathollil Kumara Menon, and their children. They used to come to our village three or four times a year in their black Ford. Their favourite pastime was visiting temples. So every time they arrived, they would have many kinds of prasadam to distribute to all of us. There would be aravanappayasam, the special sweet offered to Vishnu and Ayyappan, panchamritham, red threads that had been blessed, sandalwood paste, neyyappams, vadas, bananas and jaggery. Kalyani Amma, the old woman who took care of their children, travelled everywhere with them. She had such a rough voice that I would often run away from her, thinking that she was scolding me when all she was doing was talking to me. Sarada Oppu had three children: Krishnakumari, Rajeshwari, who was called Roji, and Vijayan. Roji had just lost her front teeth and had an unforgettably winning smile. Once when Sarada Oppu came, Roji was not with her. While we were in the outhouse, Ammamma told me in a very soft voice that she had died.

'Has Roji gone to heaven?' I asked.

Ammamma nodded.

I wanted to know who had shown Roji the way to heaven. And whether she had walked there . . .

Ammamma wiped her eyes and nose with the end of her mundu.

'Go and study,' she said.

Around that time, Rugmini, the younger sister of our playmate Radha, died too. I was very curious to know more about death. But the women of Nalapat refused to discuss the matter. It was Kannathu Unnimayamma who finally gave me a vague idea about death. She told me that the tongue protruded out of one's mouth when one died and the eyes popped out of their sockets. 'And then it comes, the last frantic breath, like the deafening thump of a drum,' she said.

'Have you seen anyone die, Unnimayamma?' I asked.

'Of course I have! Whenever I hear that someone's dying, I hurry to their house. I know how to do everything that has to be done: close the eyes, tie the feet together, close the mouth and so on. Everyone else just looks on— they've no idea what to do,' she said.

'Will those who live at Nalapat die?' I asked.

'You die when you have to, child. The God of Death has a book with all our names written in it. The time of death is entered in it too.'

'Will my name be in it, Unnimayamma?'

'Of course! There's absolutely no doubt that your name will be there, child.'

'Ammamma's name too?'

'Yes, Ammamma's too.'

'No, Ammamma's name *won't* be there,' I said, raising my voice.

Unnimayamma laughed. 'And isn't Kochu Amma, your Ammamma, a human being? Once you're born, how can you not die? Why are you getting angry with me, child? I'm not the God of Death, am I? I'm not the one who comes on a buffalo, brandishing a rope . . .'

There was a death at Nalapat that year. Ammalu Muthassi, the grandmother who had been bedridden for three years because of palsy, died. Her body lay covered in

the vadikkini for a while. Then it was taken away to the
southern yard to be cremated. No one wept.

I had thought that Ammalu Muthassi would stand up
in the pyre and fly into the sky. But I didn't see her do
anything like that.

❖

As soon as lunch was over, the new Ottam Thullal performer
went into the small room on the north-west of the verandah
at Ambazhathel and began to paint the manola mask on
his face. Malathikutty took me to Ambazhathel to watch
him dance.

The drummer set out the accessories and make-up on
the table and asked, 'Do you want some buttermilk,
Appunni Etta?'

'No. I've just eaten a full lunch. Just bring me some
cold water.'

The newcomer was different from the man who usually
performed at Punnayoorkulam. He was slim and fair, with
shoulder length hair. His teeth, though slightly irregular,
were very attractive.

'Do you know what story I'm performing today?' he
asked without taking his eyes off the mirror.

We did not reply.

'Children, it's you I'm asking!'

'We don't know,' said Malathikutty.

'The *Kalyana Sougandhikam*.'

He gathered his hair, tucked it into a towel and secured
it over his head. Then he adjusted his crown and peered
into the mirror again.

'Don't you know the story of the *Kalyana Sougandhikam*?'

'No,' we said.

'Aai, aai! Imagine the children of such a prestigious taravad not knowing this story! Don't tell anyone you don't know—it's shameful!'

'Isn't it the story of a monkey?' asked Malathikutty.

'Not just any monkey, it's the story of Hanuman himself. Of how Bhimasenan picked up his club and went to pluck the kalyana sougandhikam flower for Panchali. Don't you know who Panchali is?'

'Yes, we do.'

'The most beautiful woman in the seven worlds. The wife of the five Pandavas. A queen. It's not enough to say she was the most beautiful woman in the world—do you know what she was like, children?'

'No,' I said. Malathikutty grimaced. She'd already taken a step out of the room.

'Whom can I cite as an example of the most beautiful woman in the world? A woman like that would certainly not have been born here in Punnayoorkulam. This is such a godforsaken place. Some people call it Vanneri. Who knows which name is right? Anyway, I don't think you can find a real beauty here. You have to go to Thrissur to find beautiful women. They say all you have to do is go to the Vadakkunannathan temple early in the morning. Krishnan Namboodiri told me that you would mistake the girls who come to worship there for celestial maidens. The Namboodiri said, "Look Appunni, if you're bent on marrying a beauty, go to Thrissur. There's an army of girls who come to worship at the Vadakkunannathan temple and the Bhagavathi temple at Paramekkavu. An army, I tell you! They look like goddesses. You must go to Thrissur, you must!"'

'Are you married?' I asked the Ottam Thullal dancer.

'Why, do you want to marry me, child?'

I suddenly felt as if my ears and neck were burning. I held Malathikutty's hand tightly.

'Let's go,' said Malathikutty.

The Thullal performer laughed aloud. He had his crown on and his eyes were red. 'Are you afraid of me? I don't eat children, you know. What's your name, child?'

'Kamala!'

'You're Nalapat Balamani Amma's daughter, aren't you?'

'Um.'

'Will you give me your bangle, child? I'll wear it on my hand in your memory. Won't you give it to me?'

'Don't give him anything,' said Malathikutty.

'She's a Nalapat child. She won't refuse anything she's asked. Will you give me the bangle, child?'

I took off the bangle and gave it to him—a black plastic bangle. The Thullal dancer tried over and over again to slip it on his left hand. Finally, he succeeded.

'It looks better on my hand than on yours. I'm fairer than you, child,' he said.

'Let's go,' said Malathikutty loudly, gripping my hand.

'The bangle suits me, doesn't it, child? Isn't my hand beautiful? It looks good, doesn't it?'

We hurried into the house.

'I hate him. Did you see his look? I think he's a scoundrel!' said Malathikutty.

During the performance, the man deliberately tried to belittle us. He stared at us pointedly when he sang the line where Bhimasenan orders the monkey lying in his path to move away. The boys noticed and laughed.

At night, I asked Ammamma, 'Do I look like a monkey?'

'Why do you ask such silly questions, Kamala?'

'What do I look like?'

'Like a nice little girl.'

'Who is more beautiful: I or Panchali? I mean the Panchali who wanted the kalyana sougandhikam. Tell me, who is more beautiful?'

'Shiva, Shiva, what questions this child asks! What is it you want, Kamala? Did someone say you're not good-looking? What happened?'

I buried my face in Ammamma's blouse and sobbed. I was not quite sure why I wept so bitterly.

The next day, Malathikutty told Ammamma about the bangle. Ammamma was furious.

'Take the bangle off a child's hand? What does he mean?'

'He asked me for it and so I gave it.'

'What right has he to ask? The greedy fellow! The slovenly rascal! The old Thullal performer was such a decent sort. We won't let this one perform here any more.'

When he danced at Nalapat, the Thullal performer didn't take the kind of liberties he'd taken with us at Ambazhathel. Afraid he might provoke Ammaman to anger, he performed with great concentration. The performance he gave at Nalapat at dusk was a Sheethankan Thullal. He danced it because Ammaman had told him to.

'I'm not very familiar with it. If Narayana Menon wants it, I have to do it,' he said while he dressed. He didn't bind his waist with sashes to make it fuller for the Sheethankan Thullal. He just wrapped a dotted mundu around himself. Oil lamps were placed on the ground and hung from the ceiling as well and his costume looked marvellous in their glow. The servant woman pinched me from time to time and murmured, 'Like Devendran himself, isn't he, child?'

Ammaman gave him seven silver rupee coins and Ammayi a mundu. Ammaman asked him to come again during the Onam season.

'You must perform the Parayan Thullal then.'

'I'll have to wear a skirt made of palm leaves for that. I've never performed it. But I will if you insist, Narayana Menon.' Ammamma wrapped up a whole pile of betel leaves and a wad of tobacco for his father. The dancer joined his palms in deep obeisance.

I hoped the Thullal performer would look at me and say goodbye as he went out of the gate. And that he would give me at least a smile in return for my bangle.

His father and the drummer walked northwards hurriedly. He slowed down and said something to the servant woman standing at the fence and she said something in reply. As he walked along the edge of the field and disappeared from view, the servant woman came up to me. Beads of sweat lay along her upper lip and her body smelt of sweat.

'He's no Devendran; he's just an ordinary man,' I said.

The servant woman laughed.

'A real wily fellow he is! He says I'm the most beautiful woman in the world! I'm sure he's making fun of me.'

'And what did you say when he said that?'

'I told him not to mock poor people. What else could I say, child?'

'Malathikutty said he's a scoundrel!'

'Malathikutty has brains; she's not a fool like you, child. There's no one you don't trust. Malathikutty is right: he's a real scoundrel. I knew as soon as I saw his shifty look . . .'

❖

I remember studying in a higher elementary school called the Eliyangat School. It was around the time I left Calcutta and Achan was trying to have me enrolled in a convent school in Thrissur. The time Ammamma used to keep asking the rounded pillars in the thekkini and the temple pigeons that fluttered from time to time on to the verandah how V.M. Nair, my father, could be so hard-hearted as to leave behind a small child among strangers in Thrissur. Muthassi, Valiamma and Cheriamma did not approve at all of the plans constantly being made for my education.

'She's only a little child after all. Suppose she has nightmares?' my guileless Muthassi asked Ammamma. She had a firm conviction that bad dreams were precursors to every illness in the world.

'Don't you remember how Kochu had convulsions? She was only two at the time. She went to bed on Friday night as usual and began to scream at daybreak. No matter how much we asked, she wouldn't say anything to us. I was really frightened. I was afraid some reptile had crept out from the makeshift bathroom and stung her. We took off her clothes, laid her on the ground and examined her thoroughly. There wasn't even a scratch on her. She bent her body like a bow and screamed and screamed! Madhava Menon of Ambazhathel woke up and came over. He used to practise a bit of medicine at the time. When Valiamma had severe acidity of the stomach, it was Madhava Menon who advised us to grind asafoetida and rub it on her stomach. She improved in two hours, you know.'

Only we children were eager to listen to Muthassi's long drawn-out stories. The others had housework to do or books to read or something to study. Everyone considered Muthassi's innocence a sign of poor intelligence. She demanded nothing for herself. Born the daughter of the wealthy and ostentatious Valia Thampuran of the Punnathur Kota family, she had been decked in jewels and taken in procession on an elephant around the temple on the occasion of her kettukalyanam. In spite of all this,

Muthassi had never established for herself the place destiny had allotted her in a life of pomp and show. She never learned the language that money spoke. Nor did she care to listen to the greedy multitude around her scream and cry for wealth. When the nineteen-year-old Ammukutty picked up her only child, her daughter Kochu, and arrived at Nalapat in a palanquin with her attendants, no questions were asked of her.

'I'm not going back to the kovilakam. Let Kochu grow up here.'

It was the homecoming of a proud and dignified woman. Abandoning her husband and the security that went with preparing his bed for him, this beautiful young girl had made up her mind that the simple meal with sambhar and kalan usually served at Nalapat was enough for her. She was a woman who longed to liberate herself from the shackles of marriage, to free herself from the authority of a man. Not a single eyebrow was raised at Nalapat. Not a single face darkened. Much later, when, as a young woman, I longed to learn the first lessons in love, I pleaded with Muthassi to tell me about the time she had abandoned her husband and come away. She burst out laughing.

'I could not forgive him, that's all,' she said.

Even when she grew old, Muthassi's body remained beautiful. She was like a shrivelled little doll fashioned in gold. In her last years, a mark the size of a quarter anna appeared on her right cheek. Her eyes darted here and there as quickly, as bewitchingly, as a parrot's. Her hair smelled of oil and her toes were always immaculately free of stains.

'Were you a beauty?' I asked her.

'I had heavy gold necklaces. I wore a thick bracelet and *Ramayanam*-engraved bangles on my left hand and Mangalapuram bangles set with corals on my right. My

big traditional earrings had green stones at the centre.
When I went to the Govindapuram temple to worship on
Ekadashi day, the earrings fell off. The young girls from
Marath were making offerings of sacred platters that day,
which is why I went. Madappilayi Sankunni Nair came
with us. And a child from Kalpanchery followed—I can't
remember whether it was Keshavan or Narayanan.
Kalyani Amma from Ambazhathel had come to worship
that day. All those who saw her arrive with a tattooed
forehead, a ruby nose ring, a kuzhiminni necklace set with
white stones and twenty-four Mangalapuram bangles on
her hand were stunned. Everyone in the village knew that
Madhava Menon had gone to Chittoor and brought back
a wife who was a ravishing beauty. But he was the sort
who believed that taking women out brought the taravad
a bad name. So he had allowed her to visit the temple only
well after her youth had gone. A man must have wealth.
And a woman must have great beauty. The feudal lords of
the time believed that it was impossible to have a perfect
married life without these two important possessions.'

Muthassi's thampuran never came to her father,
Nalapat to ask her forgiveness even though he knew he
was at fault. He did not even write her a letter.

Ammamma arrived in a palanquin clinging to her
feminist mother's belly. The little girl who had to learn to
live with her physical resemblance to her father, the
Chiralayam prince. The child who had to endure having a
face as pale as the moon, a plump body, large eyes and an
indefinable odour to her perspiration. The daughter who
received as gifts from her father only an ordinary chain and
his framed photograph. Ammamma was no feminist but
she was extremely feminine. Which must have been why
she discovered heaven itself in her husband's demonstrations

of affection and in attending to his needs. Her lack of courage, her helplessness, her weakness: it was all these that drew the Chittanjoor Valia Thampuran close to her. He was thoroughly male. What he needed was a sweet-natured and soft-spoken wife.

I was born after Ammamma became a widow. She used to constantly say, 'You must never say anything offensive to your husband.' I would ask, 'What does "offensive" mean?'

'That you mustn't say anything offensive, that's all.'

'Suppose I say something offensive without knowing it's offensive?'

'That can't happen. You must live your life thinking of your husband as God.'

'Ammamma, did you worship Muthassan? Did you call him God?'

'Go and have a bath now, Kamala. Children shouldn't hang around idling in the house all the time. Or go and study.'

'I'm fed up with studying. I've already learned everything I need to know. I want to get married. To a very handsome thampuran. With a sandal paste mark on his forehead. I'm fed up with school.'

Full of dissatisfaction, I lay down with my head on her lap.

'You're crazy, Kamala. Don't say things like that in front of your uncle. It's shameful for little girls to speak like that.'

'I think I'm old enough to get married.'

'What makes you think that?'

'When I look at Marathattil Aniyan and Ambazhathel Unniettan and Govinda Kurup of our school, I feel I should get married.'

'Che, che! What crazy things this Kamala says! You're just going to be seven, child. Does anyone get married at seven? You have to be at least fifteen to get married. If you marry now, all the boys you mentioned will have to put you in a cradle and rock you to sleep. They'll have to roll rice into little balls and feed you. They'll have to take off your clothes and give you a bath. And in the end, they'll say, we don't want such a young wife; we want a wife who can make us rice and sambhar, a wife who can open a barred door.'

'That's enough, Ammamma. I don't want to hear any more. So no one will want to marry me, huh?' Ammamma gathered me in her arms, lay down and began to sing, 'Clap, clap, clap your hands . . .'

'You feel sleepy as soon as you hear music, don't you, Kamala?' asked Muthassi. 'We'll get her married to a bhagavathar—that's what we'll do.'

'That cross-eyed bhagavathar? The one who comes to our house to ask for money? He's an old man, Ammamma, isn't he? If you get me married to an old man, I'll die.'

'Old men are best, Kamala.' Muthassi chewed on her liquorice. 'They'll lie down in a corner and go to sleep. Old men won't give you problems. It's when you marry a young man that you'll have to weep all the time.'

'So V.M. Nair will have to go looking for an old man now, won't he? What about our Madappilayi Sankunni Nair? Or Channathel Narayanan Nair who acted as Kali in a play long ago?' Ammamma lay on my mattress and rolled over and over, laughing. She always went red in her ears and cheeks when she laughed.

'I'll tell you what we'll do. We'll get our Ambazhathel Das to marry the girl. He's always coming here to frighten us, dressed up as an old man with a false beard and all.

We'll write and tell him to come on leave when Kamala is here.'

'Ayyo, no! Isn't he the one whose mouth smells of onions? No, don't send for Dasettan. He always eats idlis with onion sambhar and comes and talks to me with his mouth next to my face. I want someone who doesn't eat onions.'

'So it's a Namboodiri or a Thampuran you want, is it?'

'Back to square one then. You don't have to go very far to find a Namboodiri. We can ask at the Kattumadom residence. They're relatives of old standing as well . . .'

Ammamma and Muthassi could not stop laughing.

Then Ammamma said, 'When will this child grow up? She says whatever comes to mind. I sometimes think she's too immature for her age. What foolish things she asks me!'

'A convent is the best place for her. And Madhavan Nair will have his wish as well. He thinks she'll never be modern enough if she lives here, doesn't he?'

'If you're going to teach me to be modern, I'll kill myself. I'll jump from the verandah. Suicide.'

'Who taught you that word, child?'

'Nambidi Master.'

'Nambidi? Is he mad—to ask little children to kill themselves? How horrible these teachers are! Maybe we should just arrange for the child to have lessons at home.'

❖

The moment my father's aunt, my Cheriamma, Vadekkara Narayani Amma, arrived at Nalapat, with a man carrying her basket and a gunny-cloth bag with a picture of Gandhiji on it, she called out loudly, 'Where's my Grinning Beauty?'

This was the name Cheriamma had given me. So I jumped down from the swing and ran to the southern verandah.

Cheriamma was seated on the ground, leaning against the wall to ease her tired limbs. The bright, wide smile that usually faded only when she was asleep lit up her face. Her mouth was full of the small white teeth that the dentist, Dr Kuruvilla, had made for her after extracting the big ones she used to have. The new teeth didn't show when she smiled.

She was a stout, fair, old woman, with a gigantic, Bhima-like build. Patches of white scalp were visible between her thin strands of hair. Cheriamma used a small switch of false hair, made of what she said was a deer's mane, to strengthen her natural hair. After her bath, when she sat on the verandah in the mellow sunlight, she would lay it out on the floor to sun. Thinking it would smell of a deer, I once held it to my nose. But it smelled of sesame oil heated with peppercorns. I remembered all this as soon as I saw Cheriamma.

Balan, the young man who had come with her—a good-natured boy who drifted through life with unusually large teeth that gave everyone the mistaken impression that he was smiling happily even when he grieved—shook my hand and smiled with real pleasure.

'You've grown so thin! Always going on the swing, or playing, are you?' he asked.

'What's in the basket?' I asked.

'Call Unni; I'll open it when he comes. Be patient till then, my Grinning Beauty,' said Cheriamma.

'Cheriamma's here,' I shouted.

Ammaman came running from the front verandah, Ammamma and the grandmothers from the thekkini, my Cheriamma from the southern room upstairs, the cook from the kitchen and the servant women from the southern yard. That was how loud I could shout!

Only my elder brother, who was sitting in his study in the gatehouse, studying geography, didn't come out to welcome Cheriamma. Because he was with Chami Iyer, who took tuition classes for us half an hour every day. He would make me repeat the multiplication tables in Malayalam and then say, 'Go and play now, Aami. Let me teach Mohanan.'

'When did you set out, Narayani Amma?' asked Ammaman. Everyone knew she had walked all the way from Guruvayoor. They also knew that to reach Nalapat at nine she would have had to leave Vadekkara house at least at seven. Still, politeness demanded that not only Ammaman but everyone else who was there ask Cheriamma, 'When did you set out?'

'I wanted to leave as soon as I had gone to the temple. But that didn't happen. When I finished my bath, Echmu brought me idlis and coffee. She insisted that I couldn't walk all of six miles on an empty stomach. Then this fellow here wanted to have his breakfast too. And you know he's not the sort to eat quickly. He ate his away steadily through eight idlis. And so, it was seven by the time we reached the gate of the Variam. David Doctor was taking a walk. I asked him the time and he looked at his watch. "It's seven, Narayani Amma," he said. "Where are you off to at this time of day?" "If all of you can wander around as you please, why can't I? I don't believe in that *na stree swathanthryam arhathi*—women don't merit freedom— business," I replied. Do you know what he said? "One has only to look at you, Narayani Amma, to know you don't believe in it!"'

Everyone laughed loudly.

'Unnimaya, go to Ambazhathel and tell them Cheriamma's here,' said Ammamma. Like us, everyone at Ambazhathel, adults and children, had been waiting impatiently for Cheriamma. The week she spent at Punnayoorkulam was like festival time for all of us, for our relatives, our servants and everyone.

Keshavettan, the karanavan of Ambazhathel, once said, 'When Narayani Amma is here, it's like seeing a play and a Chakyar Koothu performance all at once!' Cheriamma could mimic the way people walked and talked to perfection. She would do imitations of the madwoman who believed that an evil spirit had entered her by way of her right shoulder, of Snake-Govindan and of the Kolathappulli Namboodiri for us.

When I saw a statue of the laughing Buddha many, many years later, I was struck by the resemblance that Cheriamma bore to it in build. It was that Buddha's boat-like smile that perpetually illumined Cheriamma's flushed face.

When Cheriamma came to visit, Ammamma and I would move from the central room to the northern one. This was because only the platform in the toilet next to the central room was strong and wide enough to bear Cheriamma's weight. Cheriamma needed to get up and urinate at least ten times a night. Whenever she stayed with us, I would hear someone dipping a mug into the pot of water in the toilet every time I woke up at night.

Cheriamma was like a factory that never took a holiday: she made people laugh constantly all day and poured water to wash out the toilet all night!

All the same, she looked very healthy. She always wore pristine white: a mundu and veshti that had been starched and whitened with blue, and a white blouse. She liked upper cloths with green borders. Her clothes smelled of the smoke that rose from mattipasha, the fragrant resin that was burned like incense. I used to climb on to her lap and bury my face between her breasts, just to savour that fragrance. Cheriamma would push my face down between her ample breasts and kiss my forehead affectionately.

'You must marry our Appunni when you grow up,' she said to me once. 'You must tell your father that you insist on having Appunni Ettan as your husband.'

I didn't offer her an opinion in reply. Appunni Ettan was my father's only sister's only son. Cheriamma considered him her own son and loved him deeply.

'Why don't you say something? Don't you want to marry Appunni Ettan?' asked Cheriamma.

'Wait till I'm ten and then I'll get married. By that time Appunni Ettan would have married someone else,' I said.

'She's not as innocent as she looks,' said Cheriamma to Balan. 'She's a deep one!'

Balan smiled. Balan's sole duties were to smile and to follow Cheriamma wherever she went. In return for this generosity, Cheriamma had promised to talk to Kuttan some day and ask him to get Balan a job in Calcutta.

One day Ammamma asked Balan, 'So how far has it progressed—your attempt to get a job in Calcutta?' Cheriamma had gone for a bath and so Balan had an occasion to speak openly.

'I'm not at all sure I'll get a job. I'm not sure Kuttettan will do what Cheriamma asks. Anyway, I can't bear to think of leaving Cheriamma and going away. My own mother doesn't care for me as much as she does! I feel I'll never be able to leave Vadekkara until Cheriamma's days are over. That's how it is!'

Balan's teeth would flash a white smile even when he spoke of sad things. I found this inexpressibly attractive. I understood even then that ugliness could be as attractive as beauty.

Cheriamma had come, as she always did, with her usual basket of eatables. As Chami Iyer was about to leave after Ettan's class, Cheriamma called out, 'Wait a minute, Master. I've brought you something.'

Master blew his nose, wiped his hand on the wall and smiled at Cheriamma.

Cheriamma held out a small box. Master took it from her without touching her hand. He turned it over and over, then nodded his head eagerly.

'It's just the gift for me!' he said.

'Let's test it,' said Cheriamma. 'You're sure to sneeze a hundred and one times!'

Master opened the box, helped himself to a pinch of snuff, inhaled it and began to sneeze noisily at once. His face grew steadily redder as he sneezed. I was afraid he would die of sneezing. Cheriamma sat down, leaned against the wall and laughed delightedly every time Master bent his head and raised it to sneeze.

'Have you had enough, Master?' she asked.

'Quite, quite enough, Narayani Amma! What kind of snuff is this . . . [sneeze] . . . it's very strong. It's like inhaling powdered pepper!' Master said, perspiring.

'It's the snuff that Nattukotta Chettys use. Only they can bear its potency. You're all shaken, Master! Will you have some buttermilk?'

'No, I'll go home and eat something,' said Master.

Ettan and I set out everything from the basket on a grass mat after Master left. There were vattakanni murukkus, laddoos made by a Brahmin woman, dates, puffed rice, sweet neyyappams fried in ghee and little balls of sandalwood. Cheriamma distributed the sandalwood balls one by one. My Cheriamma, Ammayi and Ammaman's mother got one each. Then she undid a knot at her waist and handed me a small black object. 'It's excellent anjanam, antimony. Rub it on a chana-stone and line your eyes with it. They'll look so beautiful.'

When I turned the piece of antimony over and looked at it, I thought I saw white lines running through it. That evening, while I was playing in the courtyard at Ambazhathel, Prasanna's father, Kunhunni Ettan, called me to him.

'Prasanna told me that Narayani Amma gave you some anjanam,' he said. 'Don't put it in your eyes. It's poison. You'll fall ill if it gets into your bloodstream.'

I never used the piece of antimony. It lay useless in the tin box in which Ettan kept stamps, coins and marbles.

When I was eight, Cheriamma fell ill and took to bed in the room on the south in Vadekkara. I visited Vadekkara once while going back to boarding school in Thrissur. I heard a terrible scream from the room and was terrified. Balan put his head out and said, 'Don't be afraid, Aami— it's only Cheriamma. She's in agony because her bowels haven't moved for three days now. It hurts so much that she can't sleep, day or night.'

I hid behind my father's sister.

'Don't you want to see Cheriamma?' asked Balan.

I felt my legs giving way. My palms were sweating. 'Bring her here, Balan,' commanded Cheriamma in a man's voice.

'I don't want to see Cheriamma,' I said.

❖

I was eight years and eight months old when my mother had another baby, a girl. Those were the days when a midwife was brought to stay in the house around the time a woman was expected to deliver. The midwife became my mother's constant companion during that period. She was a Syrian Christian. The people at Nalapat called her 'Nurse' or 'Nice'. All the usual caste taboos were conveniently set aside at the time of childbirth.

Nurse enjoyed her stay at Nalapat. She only had to open her mouth to speak, and she would find willing listeners. She had a comfortable room too.

'A plate of fish curry and life would be bliss!' she said to the servants. The servants smiled sympathetically, being, like her, meat-eaters forced to subsist on a vegetarian diet.

It was Valli who found a solution. Lunch was usually over at Nalapat at one o'clock. After that, Nurse began to go to Mambulli house to chew betel. It was not that the Nalapat folk would not give her betel leaves and areca nuts and the tobacco they had pounded themselves at home, but Nurse insisted on chewing only country tobacco. She quickened her pace as she walked to Mambulli. Once she arrived there, she sat down on a low stool in the front verandah and helped herself to a meal of excellent unbroken rice and sardine curry cooked in tamarind. Afterwards, she chewed betel mixed with good country tobacco to cleanse her mouth of the smell of fish. I enjoyed these little ruses very much. When she set out on her mission, her cloth umbrella unfurled, I would follow her until the pond, looking at her figure draped in a starched sari, full until the waist and then very slender. I liked watching the way she stuffed her mouth with food and the way she spat betel juice into the bushes. I also loved her loud, noisy laugh.

It was customary at the time to give a pregnant woman castor oil as she neared the time of her confinement. An

auspicious day was first found and she was given the
purgative the day before. The baby usually arrived the
day after the purging. So, in the month of Vrischikam, on
the day of the Uthradam star, Amma was asked to take
her castor oil. Muthassi announced that the baby would
be born either the next day, on Thiruvonam, or the day
after, on Avittam. But the baby came only three days later,
on the day the Poororuttadi star was in the ascendant.

I woke up suddenly in the middle of the night and saw the
verandah brightly lit. People were talking in low voices in
the central hall. I was not sure whether it was all right to go
there and find out what was happening. I knew that only
grown-ups could participate in events that happened at night.

I heard the nurse's voice clearly. She was saying, 'Strain
now. Push hard again . . .'

I thought it funny and bit my pillow to stifle my
laughter. Then I fell asleep again.

When I woke up, Ammamma was calling out, 'Kamale,
Kamale, get up!' The sky beyond the window was still
dark and I was surprised that Ammamma was telling me
to get up.

'Don't you want to see your little sister, Kamala?' she
asked.

'Has my little sister arrived?'

'Yes!'

I went to the central room with my eyes half closed, as
if going to see the Vishukkani, the first glowing vision of
the Malayalam New Year. Amma was lying on her side,
asleep. On the floor, a red-hued infant lay on a mat. There
were drops of blood on the tip of its umbilical cord. The
smell of Dettol hung heavily in the air.

'Don't you want to touch your little sister?' asked
Ammamma.

'Not just now.'

'Don't you like her, Kamala?'

I nodded my head.

'When will this child be big enough to play with me?' I asked.

Ammamma smiled.

'She won't ever play with you. By the time she grows big, you'll have stopped playing, Kamala.'

'Then why did Amma have this baby?'

'Don't say silly things, Kamala. Go and brush your teeth and do your lessons.'

While we were having breakfast, Ettan said, 'I can put that baby in my pocket—it's so tiny. Shall I try?'

'It won't go into your pocket. It'll go in your school bag. What about the squirrel you said you would tame? You've been talking about it for so long and you haven't even caught one!'

He had always wanted to tame a squirrel and make it his companion. Preparing cardboard boxes for it, drilling small holes in them, searching for mousetraps: these were all part of his everyday routine those days. He told me he knew squirrel-language. 'He's bragging!' said Marathattil Aniyan. No one in our village could make Aniyan believe anything. He wouldn't even believe us when we told him Rabindranath Tagore was dead. I had watched Tagore's funeral procession go past the windows of our house in Calcutta. But Aniyan would only say, 'Go on, Aami, you're just making it up!'

There were two types of people in our village at that time: a group who thought of truth as lies and another that thought of lies as truth. Both groups were entangled in a web of fallacy.

The nurse stayed on at Nalapat for a week after the baby was born. Amma and Ammamma gave her gifts: a sari, slippers, a leather bag and so on. Both she and Unnimayamma liked helping Amma with her bath. But Amma would not allow them in the bathroom.

'I'll rub oil on your body,' Unnimayamma would suggest.

'I can manage on my own,' Amma would say.

The nurse and Unnimayamma would sit on the eastern verandah, outside the bathroom, while Amma had her bath. I would sit near them too to listen to their conversation.

'This is an English way of having a baby,' said Unnimayamma. 'Now, the real care given to a woman who's having a baby is a sight to see! First you rub Dhanvantharam oil over her body, then some raw turmeric. They have to be rubbed in for half an hour. After that, you apply green gram powder to remove the oil and wash it away with bright red water that has been boiled with thechhi leaves. Then you give her some garlic paste to eat, along with powdered fennel seeds. I know how to make all these. But they didn't want any of it. If the body isn't taken care of properly now, it will go to seed. But what's the use of my saying that? No one wants to listen.'

'She'll have English medicines. Tonics and all that. Whoever eats garlic paste and powdered fennel now? V.M. Nair will send her whatever medicines she needs from Calcutta.'

'And what medicines can you get in Calcutta? Do they get medicines we don't have here? Last year, I attended on a woman who had a baby here. She took three medicines regularly: a thick lehyam to make her hungry, another one to make her thirsty and a third to improve her health.

Do you know what colour her skin became after she had the baby? The colour of a newly minted gold sovereign! And her figure? What can I say—I was afraid someone would cast an evil eye on her when she went to the temple, she was so lovely! Like a goddess!'

The nurse examined her own unattractive hands with care.

'They're chapped,' she said. 'Do they have freshly made sesame seed oil here? I need an oil bath.'

'Come with me to the pond. I'll oil your back for you.'

'You must have seen a lot of childbirths, Unnimayamma . . .?'

'No baby is born is this village without my being there. That's the truth. I never enter low caste houses. I go to Nair houses and Namboodiri ones. They say that if the apothecary doesn't see me, he asks, "Where is Unnimayamma?" He told me that it gives him strength to have me there to help. He loves cracking jokes. But sometimes he'll say, do you want the mother or the child, *you* have to decide. He'll say he can save only one of them. There'll be much beating of breasts then and wailing and they'll all fall at the apothecary's feet, saying, save them both! Sometimes he does. Sometimes he extracts the child, cutting it away from the mother. It's unbearable to watch! If it's a boy, there's a pretty little penis. All lacerated with a knife, a mess of blood. It makes me dizzy sometimes. But I never have time to even sit down, you know. They're all Guruvayoorappan's games, aren't they, Nurse?' The nurse nodded.

'A mess of blood? Where does the blood come from?' I asked Unnimayamma, frantic with anxiety. My legs trembled with fear.

'Oh God, has this child been here all the time, listening to all this? Guruvayoorappa, Kochu Amma will scream at

me! Go away and play, child. Don't hang around when
grown-ups are talking. Can't you go and play on the front
verandah? Look at your brother: learn from him how
to behave. He's such a good boy, always reading.
Or writing.'

'Why does this child behave this way? Sitting here and
listening to us talk about women having babies! Go and
play now. I've no time to talk to you, child. I've got work
to do.'

❖

Every Monday evening, my unmarried Cheriamma would
sit down by the pillar in the thekkini and read the
Mathrubhumi weekly aloud. Her listeners were me, Ettan,
Ammamma and the grandmothers. When a short story by
Pottekkat or Uroob was published, we would all sit in the
thekkini holding our breath, numb with anxiety as we
waited for the end of the story. Someone once wrote a
love story about scorpions. Sri Madhavan's illustrations
made that story more enchanting. My brother and I
enjoyed it. The grandmothers did not like it all that much.
They pretended it was part of their nature to dislike love
stories. Ammamma would often say disgustedly, 'Pure love
indeed! It repels me to hear the word!' The women of
Nalapat believed that women from good taravads should
be scornful of love.

❖

We must have been back from Calcutta for about a week
when a parcel came by post for the maidservant. This
happened many years ago and I don't remember there being
a postman in the village at that time. Rappayi, the

postmaster's servant, used to come late in the evening to Nalapat with letters and magazines. When Rappayi arrived at dusk one day, he had a parcel with him. A packet wrapped in unbleached cloth with wax seals on three sides. It was addressed to our maidservant. Ammaman read her name out and said, 'There's no one here by that name.'

Ammamma put her head out of the kitchen door and said, 'There is. It's our servant woman.'

'It's a parcel,' Rappayi called out. 'A parcel from Calcutta. You have to sign for it. Or smear ink on your thumb and make a thumb impression.'

The maidservant was in the kitchen, holding bangle bits to the fire to bend them. When she heard all this commotion, she began to cry.

'She won't come out. You sign for it, Kuttan,' said Ammaman's mother.

I saw Ammamma go red in the face. She cut the knot on the parcel with a kitchen knife. Two freshly washed mundus with gold thread borders slid to the ground. And a letter from the cook in Calcutta.

'Why has he sent you mundus?' Ammamma asked.

The servant woman hid behind a heap of jackfruits that had been piled up to ripen in a dark corner just beyond the door of the vadikkini.

'Why has he sent you mundus?' Ammamma asked again.

'I don't know,' said the servant woman.

'I'm going to send them back tomorrow,' said Ammamma. She crumpled up the cook's letter without even reading it and threw it into the kitchen fire.

'I haven't done anything wrong. I swear by the Bhagavathi of the Punnorkkavu, I haven't done anything wrong,' wailed the servant woman.

The grandmothers suggested that the girl be sent back to her house. But she beat her breast and wailed and the decision was deferred.

From that day, the servant woman began to behave' like the repentant Mary Magdalene. She stopped going to the river with the other girls for a bath. She would sit for hours with my baby sister on her lap, looking sorrowfully into empty space.

'I'll never go back to Calcutta, child,' she said to me.

'Why?'

'I have a good reason. But I can't tell you—you're a child.'

One day, she told Amma about a rich landlord who had been threatening her. He had warned her that he would burn down her house if she didn't give in to him.

'What does he want?' I asked her.

'I can't tell children all that.'

I told Ammamma about this and she was very angry.

'The wretch! We should have sent her away long ago. She should remember there are children growing up here.'

One afternoon, her mother came to Nalapat in search of her. She said relatives from Ponnani were visiting, that she needed her at home and would bring her back the next day.

That evening, Ammamma sent the cook to her house. 'Tell her to come quickly—the baby is crying.'

We had finished dinner when the cook returned. He put down the hurricane lamp on the eastern verandah and collapsed on the floor.

'I can't go on errands like this, Valiamma. Don't send me to houses of women like her. I'm so ashamed.'

'What happened?'

'When I arrived there, I heard someone coughing. So I peered in . . . Who do you think it was, Valiamme?'

'That's enough; don't tell me anything more.'

'He peered out through the window and saw me as well. I nearly died. Don't allow that girl in here any more. We have children here—she'll ruin them.'

The cook didn't eat that night.

❖

While we were in Calcutta, an old man, a Mangalorian, used to come to our house to teach my younger brother, Sundaran. The cook called him Saypu, white man, and we called him Vayaran Master, Pot-Belly Master. His stomach was as big as the whole world. When we sat down in front of him, we could hear from it the crash of thunder, the roar of the sea and the screeching of parrots. How we laughed! But Sundaran never dared to laugh. He would sit there, his face pale, listening to everything Master said.

Pot-Belly Master told us that all Hindus would starve to death if the British were driven out of India and that the concept of the Congress had taken shape from the evil thoughts of the Hindus. 'If I were the British king, I would shoot all these people. What can you do with treason-mongers except kill them?'

Sundaran gazed at Master's gestures with fear in his eyes. The servant materialized at that moment with hot tea and snacks on a tray.

'They're not the snacks you really like, Master. These are vadas and sukhiyans, local snacks. We should be giving you cakes, but we don't make cakes here since they contain eggs,' said the servant.

'Local snacks are all right—after all, I have to eat them sometimes. I'm fed up of cakes! I have them at home all the time, different kinds.' Master ate all the snacks, one by one, and the servant helped himself to a few too, from

the same plate. We kept laughing, all of us, but Sundaran's
face grew even paler.

'Why do they laugh all the time? They don't know the
fundamentals of courtesy,' Master mumbled.

The servant's face brightened like a lotus.

'That's true, Saypu. They've grown up in the village and
behave like boors. Have you heard of Punnayoorkulam,
Saypu? It's a small, godforsaken village. These children
grew up there. Now it's for you, Saypu, to teach them
manners. You must pay them special attention.'

'I don't come here to teach all these children. I come to
teach Shyamsundar. I promised to teach him all the subjects
for forty rupees. Shyamsundar is a well-behaved child.'

I told Amma that the cook had complained about us.
But Amma did not dare find fault with him.

Even as early as a week before Christmas, people would
start bringing baskets of food as gifts for Achan. Very
often, the baskets contained bottles of alcohol as well.
Achan presented the bottles to Sundaran's master. The
cook liked alcohol too. So, one day, he opened a bottle of
whisky, poured it into another container, filled it with
pepper rasam and put it back in the basket. Pot-Belly
Master discovered this bit of treachery only after he got
back home. The next day, he said, 'Poor Mr Nair! He
doesn't even realize that there are people deceiving him
all the time. People who fill bottles with pepper rasam
and label it whisky! I had a suspicion when I broke the
seal itself . . .'

Master scrutinized the cook's face when he came with
tea and vadas. His eyes were red and his lips were twisted
in a sneer. Master understood it was the cook who had
tricked him.

'Open your mouth,' Master said.

The cook laughed.

'You stink of alcohol,' said Master.

Master met Achan that evening and had a discreet talk with him for two minutes. The cook said to me, while he relaxed on the kitchen steps at dusk, smoking a beedi, 'I have a feeling this wretched Saypu will tell tales about me and do me out of my job. Where did your father find such a wicked Saypu, child? That boy is never going to better himself, learning from him, that's certain. He's all black, inside and outside. A monster! Forty rupees he's paid! For forty rupees you can get a real white Saypu to teach the children!'

It was around that time that a guru named Brajbashi began coming home to teach me Manipuri dance and a teacher named Mishra to teach me Hindi. The living room carpet was rolled up for me to learn dancing, and the door to the dining room closed. In spite of this, Pot-Belly Master would knock on the door at least a dozen times with his stick and call out, 'Stop that noise! Shyamsundar has examinations next month. Do you want him to fail?'

The dance master smiled.

'Is that old man who teaches your brother mad?' he asked me.

'I don't know.'

'A fool who has no love for dance or music—an animal!'

The dance master praised the snacks the cook had given him and shared his betel leaves and tobacco with him gladly.

'It's dangerous to let these Anglo-Indians into the house. They'll turn the children's cultural talents topsy-turvy. Poor Shyamsundar, if he stays with that teacher for a year, he'll turn into an Anglo-Indian himself! He'll even stop using water when he goes to the toilet,' warned the dance master.

'We are Hindus. We cannot survive a day without water,' said the cook.

'Aren't you a Brahmin?' asked Brajbashi.

'No, I'm a Nair,' said the cook.

'Then you must be a Kayastha; you can't be lower than that. You look as if you are from a high caste.'

The Hindi master would arrive after both the other teachers had left and the first stars were twinkling in the evening sky. Overcome with shyness, he would walk to the dining room looking down at his feet. His toes made a sound, tick-tick, as he walked, as if someone was snapping them.

The cook brought him snacks as he did for the others. But Mishra showed no interest in talking to him.

Master told me that the cook's Hindi was very mediocre, that he distorted not only the grammar disgracefully but the pronunciation as well.

'You mustn't talk to him in Hindi, Kamala,' he said.

'No, Sir, I won't.'

'And not just in Hindi, don't talk to him much in any language. You must treat servants as servants.'

'All right, Sir.'

The Hindi master's inimical manner astonished the cook. 'Why does he look so angry when he sees me? His face looks like a farting fox's! Where did they get a Hindi master like him from? Basra Mishra indeed! Even his name makes me nauseous!'

'You're jealous of him,' said the servant woman.

'Me? Jealous? Of him?' The cook's face blazed with fury.

'You don't like the way he looks at me.'

'Indeed! Who cares if some wretch stares at a servant woman from some godforsaken village? Let him look; let him marry her if he wants. Why should I care?'

That day, the servant woman cried. But the cook did not bother to go and comfort her. Before dinner, he smoked his way through a whole pack of beedis.

Amma and Achan always came down the stairs exactly at nine for dinner.

❖

The Second World War was drawing to a close. We were living in Calcutta, on the first floor of 18 Lansdowne Road . . .

Achan used to get the yellow British *Daily Mirror* and the American weekly *Saturday Evening Post* regularly in those days. Since the *Mirror* was not suitable for intellectuals, I was the only one who read it. A comic strip called *Jane* used to be published in it every day, to enthuse the soldiers. The beautiful Jane used to often appear unclothed in many places, maybe because she had forgotten to put on her clothes. It was a story with no particular plot. Her shapely, attractive body was itself the plot. The soldiers thought of Jane even when they were fighting. I read later that there were people who proclaimed that it was because of Jane that they had won the war. The *Post* had short stories and a serial called *Tugboat Annie*. This American journal assumed for me the same importance as the *Mathrubhumi* weekly used to have in Nalapat. It became a valuable treasure as I waited for the postman. I liked the pictures drawn by Norman Rockwell. He touched upon the beauty of familial concepts. Often he would have a father, a mother, a grandfather, a grandmother, a boy, a girl, a child, a dog, a cat, a horse and a parrot all in the same picture. He always tried to portray the strength and security of the American family. In those days, no one said that the American family was crumbling to pieces because of sexual anarchy. Nor did ugly men and women conduct discussions on sexual anarchy. I believed that the Americans, the Japanese, the English, the Germans and the Indians all belonged to one family. I knew nothing then of politics. Or of the capacity politics had for destruction.

The American children who arrived as guests at our neighbour's house played with us. They seemed different from us only in their food habits. I could see into their bedroom from my window. They used to lie beside their mother at night and listen to her tell stories. Ettan and I had fallen asleep so many, many times listening to Amma's stories. I thought of that time again.

It was around that time that we too had guests: Saralechi, the daughter of Professor Sankaran Nambiar; her husband, a prince belonging to the royal family of Kochi; and their son Mohan. Achan had told them they could stay with us until they found a house for themselves. It was the first time in my life that I saw a fashionable Malayali woman like Saralechi. The women of Punnayoorkulam, whether they were rich or poor, never bothered to clean their fingers. It was a common sight to see dirt under their fingernails and lice in their hair. Saralechi was fashionable as well as beautiful. She had amusing stories to relate and loved to laugh as well as make other people laugh. Besides her gold ornaments, she wore a bead chain as well.

She hummed under her breath all the time, bringing music into our rooms upstairs.

My father and mother did not enjoy talking to children very much. That must have been why I was so delighted when Saralechi asked me about my school activities. I had been looking for a model to imitate and I found one in Saralechi.

I asked Kallu, 'Will I ever be as beautiful as Saralechi some day?'

'No,' she said.

'Why not?'

'No matter how long you live, you'll never have such fair skin.'

'Can't I become beautiful without having fair skin?'

'No, child. You might have elegance. But you'll never be as beautiful as Saralamma. There's no use wishing that.'

'I don't wish it.'

'Then why did you ask me a question like that?'

'Just like that.'

Kallu laughed. She often laughed as she talked about me to the cook. She had been specially appointed to take care of my younger sister. I didn't have a servant maid of my own. Tripura, who mopped the floors in the house, slept on a mat next to my bed at night. She often told me stories. The only one I remember is the one about a monkey.

The monkey's owner was a zamindarini, a very wealthy woman who loved jewellery. Watching her put on her chain after chain studded with precious stones, the monkey grew envious. He stole them one by one and hid them behind the cowshed. He defecated on them so that they would not be visible. The zamindarini could never find her jewels. Till the rains came. The monkey's shit was washed away and the jewels became visible. The woman sold the monkey to a gypsy for two rupees. Not only this story but all Tripura's stories had a moral. I took a decision after listening to this one: I would never rear a monkey in my house!

❖

I came back again to Nalapat soon after my eleventh birthday for my summer holidays. Ammamma scrutinized me from head to foot, smiled and said, 'Next Monday I'll teach you how to wear an onnara, Kamala.' An onnara is the undergarment that Malayali women wear. Three yards long, it is wrapped around the waist first, then an end is taken up between the legs and tucked securely at the back. Ammamma's decision made me happy. I wanted my childhood to end quickly—I longed to be a young woman.

The very next day, Ammamma bought five muzhams of short-width mull and cut it up into four onnaras. Tailor Kumaran did the hems. Lakshmikutty bleached them white. My friend Malathikutty from Ambazhathel also came that Monday morning to the Nalapat thekkini to learn how to put on an onnara. Ammamma took out a pink jacket and a mundu with a thin, coloured border from her wooden box. She took both of us to the thekkini so that the servants would not see us. She showed us once how to fasten the onnara around the waist, draw it up between the legs so that it fell into fine folds at the back and tuck one end firmly into the waist at the back. Then Malathikutty and I helped each other to put it on properly.

'Does everyone wear onnaras?' I asked.

'All women born in the Nair community do. To make their waists slim. You'll never look beautiful if you don't wear an onnara.'

I thought of the women I'd seen in Calcutta, who were beautiful even though they did not wear onnaras. But I didn't dare argue with Ammamma.

'I can't wear this when I go to school,' I said. 'What if it shows under my frock? Everyone will laugh at me.'

'It's if you don't wear one that they'll laugh at you,' said Ammamma.

Wearing my onnara under my mundu, I wandered all over the Nalapat compound until the summer vacation was over. I longed to put an end to my schooldays and start my married life just as Ammamma had done. I wanted to stay on at Nalapat. I loved having oil baths, swimming in the pond, sleeping in the vadikkini upstairs all afternoon. While I was at Nalapat, Calcutta faded from my mind like an old dream. I used to feel then that Calcutta was not real, that it was Nalapat that was real. That the absolute realities of life were the thudding of the drums at the Para festival, the roar of the velichappadu as he became possessed, the songs of the Parayankaali dancers. The Kamala who lived in Calcutta, the one who spoke English and Bengali, turned into a girl who was part of a dream, the mute princess of the fairy tale.

Later, when I had to go back to Calcutta, I sat in the train holding back tears. Those were the days when a first-class compartment was meant for only four people. When all of us—Achan, Amma, I, my elder and younger brothers and my younger sister—travelled together, Achan would ask me to spread a sheet on the floor of the compartment and sleep on it. If the train jolted too much, the back of my head would hit the floor and hurt badly. Once, on a journey like this, I got up, sat at the window and looked out. Early morning, when the train stopped at a station, a madwoman came running towards me with her hands outstretched. Her teeth were chipped at the edges. Later, I used to often see that distorted smile in my dreams and wake up with a start, crying.

The madwoman called me 'meri beti', my daughter, making me feel frightened and uneasy. Ammamma used to say, 'Kamala, you're mad,' whenever I acted thoughtlessly. I really began to wonder whether I was not, after all, that madwoman's daughter.

Kunhathu, who worked as a peon in my father's firm, stayed in our house in Calcutta. Number eighteen Lansdowne

Road had six bedrooms, a drawing room and a dining room. But sixty-four-year-old Kunhathu spent his days in the room next to the coal room in the kitchen block. He often talked to me about his pretty daughter.

'Cheruchi is two years older than you, child. Her skin is fairer than yours, you know. A rosy skin, like a tomato.'

'Doesn't Cheruchi go to school?'

'She's bone lazy, that Cheruchi. Only if she's given two whacks with a broomstick will she pick up her slate and go to the Kottapadi school.'

Tripura had told us that once a woman had hanged herself in the servants' latrine. So, afraid to go there at night to urinate, Kunhathu took to urinating in the coal room, making the whole area stink.

When he heard the servant woman and the cook complain about the stink, Kunhathu said, 'There's a cat that comes here—a white tomcat. I've often woken up hearing it mew. It's that creature that pisses there. What's the point of finding fault with me for what the cat does?'

Kunhathu slept in the room next to the coal room until the cook married the servant woman. One day, the cook extended a piece of paper towards Amma with 'I love Kallu' written on it. Amma sent for Kallu and asked her what she thought of this. She said she loved him too. And that was how Amma got them married to each other without any delay in our puja room. Then she asked Kunhathu to give them his bedroom.

'Imagine that wretched woman getting married! Anyone but our Balamani Amma would have thrown out those two creatures and slammed the door on them!'

The old man gathered his belongings, his suitcase, his clothesline and a few pairs of khaki shorts, and dragged them down the stairs, muttering, 'How many times have I told Balamani Amma not to bring women from Kerala to work here! I know them only too well. They're all bad women! Not fit to set foot in decent homes!'

The next time I heard young Kallu chatting with her husband, I asked her, 'Kallu, are you a bad woman?'

'And who said that? Must be that old man! No one else would talk ill of me. Tell me the truth, child, who told you that?'

I would not let out Kunhathu's name. He always told me stories—of how he had worked in the ARP force, how he had worked as a butler for Aubrey Menen's parents and how, when Aubrey's mother, a white woman, had asked what a pineapple was, he had told her, 'Madam, that is ass-fruit.'

One day, Achan's younger brother, whom we called Appu Ettan, took all of us children to see a Hindi film called *Bandhan*. On the way back home, Kunhathu discovered that his ticket had cost six annas and beat his chest in despair, saying he could have bought seventy-two beedis for that sum. 'Or six teas. And not just tea, a half-tea with a roll of bread! Balan Nair, never drag me to a Hindi film again. Just give me the money for the ticket instead.'

Appu Ettan told us he'd never met a fellow as unpleasant as Kunhathu.

'And I'd thought he's the sort that likes cultural shows!'

❖

Our aunt, whom we all affectionately called Kutti Oppu, had a perfume called Ottodilbahaar sent to her once a year by post from Lucknow. My elder brother must have managed to get hold of an empty bottle that had contained this, for he suddenly decided he would manufacture perfume. He declared he would turn it into a big business.

When I asked him from what ingredient he would make the perfume, he said it was a secret he would reveal to no one. I was ready to cry when I heard this. Finally, after Ammamma intervened on my behalf, he consented to share the secret with me.

On the way from Nalapat to the carpenter's workshop, the ground along the edge of the paddy fields was usually scattered with flowers and seeds of the punna tree that grew by the Cheruvathoor family's fence. Ettan used to collect punna seeds to play marbles with. If you scraped off the green skin and dried them in the sun, they turned into marbles. My brother had a big, black wooden box in which he stored his glass marbles and the punna-seed marbles. He used to tell me that they would prove useful to him some day.

'You can make scent from punna seeds,' he said.

'Won't it stink?' I asked. My brother smiled mockingly, as if he despised my lack of intelligence.

'It won't stink. It will be fragrant. We can bottle it and sell it at a rupee a bottle.'

'Who will buy it?'

'Kutti Oppu. And once she buys it and uses it, other people will buy it too.'

It was a Sunday. My brother decided not to waste any time; he would start to manufacture his perfume at once. He asked me to go and gather punna seeds quickly, before Marathattil Aniyan arrived to play with us.

'Take care no one sees you gather them.'

Cheruvathoor Keshavan Nair saw me bend down and pick up the punna seeds.

'Why are you gathering these, child? Do girls play marbles?' he asked, smiling.

'I know how to play marbles,' I said.

'If you play marbles in the sand, you'll have itchy, sore fingers. Be careful. Did you see what happened to Ambazhathel Unni? His whole body itches. The washerman is treating him now. Didn't you see him walking around with a mundu smeared with sulphur wrapped around his neck? Do you want to go around like that, child, with a cloth smeared with medicine around your neck?'

'No!' I said.

'Girls shouldn't play marbles. It's not good for you to mess around in the sand. Your hands will be covered with dust. And you'll develop sores that itch. You won't be pretty any more. There'll be black scabs when the sores heal. Don't you know this, child?'

I did not say anything. I hid twelve punna seeds in the folds of my frock and ran back with them to Nalapat. Ettan called out from the toilet near the vadikkini, 'I'm here!'

Only the servant women slept in the vadikkini at night. They never used the toilet. On the windowsill of the toilet were an unframed bit of broken mirror, a kajal container and two paper packets of red and violet coloured sindooram. There were black kajal stains and red sindooram stains on the wall. I saw two jam bottles there as well, filled with water. Ettan had a penknife with a handle made of buffalo horn in his hand.

'Let's start making the scent,' he said.

'Now?'

'Close that door and bolt it. No one must see.' Ettan broke the skin and took out the punna seed inside. Then he powdered it and mixed it with the water in the jam jar. He shook the mixture for quite some time.

'This is going to be a great business—as big as the Lucknow Ottodilbahaar perfume.'

'Will our scent be just like that Dilbahaar?'

Ettan laughed. 'This is going to be called Mohandas scent,' he said.

'So it won't have my name then,' I said, disappointed.

'I won't use your name, Aami, for this one. I'll give the second one we make your name.'

We covered the bottles of perfume with a basket, left them in the toilet and went out to play. Marathattil Aniyan and Thangam were seated on the platform built around the snake shrine.

'And how far has it progressed, your scent making?' asked Aniyan. My brother and I were astonished.

'Won't punna seeds stink if you put them in water? Who will buy a perfume that stinks?' asked Aniyan.

'How did you know I was making scent?' Ettan asked.

'We hid outside the window and overheard what you said. This won't turn out to be good. Who will buy perfume that stinks?'

'I've put something in the bottle so that it won't stink,' said Ettan.

I jumped up and down and repeated, 'It's true, we put in something so that it won't stink.'

'Don't think too much of yourself, Aami, because you're making scent from punna seeds,' said Thangam, pouting.

'I'll make real scent for you, Mohanan,' said Aniyan.

'Make your own scent yourself,' said Ettan.

'We'll start a business together. I know how to make perfume from flowers. You have to gather parijatham flowers, jasmines and chembakams, soak them in oil and put it out in the sun. Strain it after three or four days and you'll have sweet-smelling perfume.'

'Have you tried it?'

'No. That Thyaganandan told me.'

'Which Thyaganandan?'

'The one who married a woman from the Kottayath family. He said he'd made it once.'

'Well, you make it yourself then. And I'll make mine.'

Aniyan and Thangam did not stay to play with us that day. They waited for a while silently, looking as if they were annoyed with us and then went back without saying a word.

'Anybody can make a perfume with flowers and you can find it in any shop. But our scent is special—you won't find it anywhere. If people want it, they'll have to come to us, won't they?' Ettan asked me.

I nodded.

Two or three days later, Devaki called out from the darkness of the vadikkini, 'Amme, there's a terrible stench here . . .'

Unnimaya, Sankaran and the others peered into the vadikkini.

'I think it's a dead rat,' said Unnimaya.

'Move those baskets and sweep the place thoroughly. Let's find out what it is that's dead,' said Sankaran.

'It doesn't smell like a dead rat; it's something else. I think it's dog shit,' said Muthassi, who had just entered the vadikkini.

'No dog's ever come in here,' said Devaki.

'The northern door's always lying open. The dogs from the washermen's quarters must have got in that way. No one listens to me!' Muthassi complained.

'If those dogs come here again, I'll throw stones at them and break their legs!' said Sankaran.

'Don't do that. If you hurt dumb creatures, you won't have to wait for your next birth, you'll reap the consequences in this life itself, Sankara.'

'This is not dog shit or cat shit,' said Devaki, thrusting her broom into the corners. 'Let's see if there's a bandicoot lying dead somewhere.'

'How can a bandicoot get into the vadikkini, Amral? It must be one of those small mice for sure,' said Unnimaya.

'The stink's coming from the vadikkini,' said Muthassi.

Ettan looked at me in despair. I went to the toilet and examined the bottles. Their tops had burst. I saw white mould floating on the water inside. And something like the fine membrane you sometimes see when you break an egg. When I held the bottle to my nose, the evil odour made all my nerves go weak.

'It's unbearable,' I said to Ettan.

'There might be people who like this scent,' said Ettan.

'The children have concocted something in these bottles here, and it's stinking,' said Unnimaya. She held up a bottle to the light. 'Look, there's something like a worm inside!'

When everyone arrived at the spot, Ettan threw the bottles angrily on to the rubbish heap outside.

'The perfume's gone now,' I lamented. 'All of you came and destroyed our business.'

Ettan summed it up, 'We tried to make perfume. And we didn't succeed. But something's come alive in that bottle. Didn't you see something white moving inside it?'

I nodded.

'That's how you make life. If we try a little harder, we can make human beings instead of worms. We need big bottles. I'll start a laboratory when I grow up to try out all kinds of experiments.'

'I'll come, too, to help you,' I said.

'You won't be able to help, Aami. Sometimes there are explosions in labs. You'll be scared if you see one.'

'Don't you need me even to collect punna seeds?' I asked tearfully.

'Why would scientists need punna seeds?' asked Ettan, laughing loudly.

❖

When I was a child, we didn't dial numbers on the telephone. If I wanted to call Achan in his office, I would take up a phone and a woman's voice would say, 'Number, please.' I would say, PK (which probably stood for Park Street, Calcutta) one-six-two-o and wait for the connection to be made.

The telephone operator in Achan's office was a middle-aged man named Bhattacharya. He had a woman's voice. I heard Appu Ettan tell his friend Pichirikkattu Balan Nair that some impudent fellows had tried to flirt with Bhattacharya under the mistaken impression that he was a woman! Appu Ettan and his friend found this very amusing. I asked Amma why they found this so funny.

'What does "flirt" mean?' I asked.

'It means saying flattering things to women about their beauty, writing descriptive verses about them and all that,' she said.

One day, while Achan was having breakfast, I asked him, 'Do you know, Achan, that people have been reciting slokams to Bhattacharya, who works at your office?'

'Reciting slokams to Bhattacharya! What nonsense! Is the child off her head?'

'It was Pichirikkattu Balan Nair and Appu Ettan who told me . . .'

Appu Ettan and Balan Nair hurried out of the house. Later that day, Appu Ettan said to me that I was not to listen when he talked to people and that if I did overhear something I was not to repeat it to Achan or Amma. 'What we speak about is not suitable for children.'

All this made me uneasy. If I arrived in the kitchen when the cook and the servant woman were talking softly to each other, one of them would say, 'Children shouldn't listen to what we're saying. Go and play outside, child.'

And if Achan and Amma were talking to each other upstairs and I arrived on the scene, Achan would say, 'Go downstairs and study. You shouldn't hang around listening to elders talk. I'll slap you if you disobey me.'

Only Kunhathu spoke of things meant for children to hear. Stretched out on his rope cot, in his net banian and khaki shorts, in the room that stank of urine, he would say to me, 'If only I could get hold of some mustard oil to massage my legs. When I wake up at night to urinate, I can hardly stand—I have such bad cramps. As if someone is pulling at my leg with ropes. Kunhathu's exhausted, child. I think I'm going to die soon. I'm seventy now. I told them at the office that I'm only sixty. I didn't want them to think I'm too old to work and dismiss me. My family in Kottapadi lives on the money I send—do you know that, child?'

Kunhathu allowed me to sit at the foot of the rope cot. After the first five or six minutes, I would feel the darkness in the room gradually lessening and be able to make out all the things around me. On the clothesline in one corner hung a shirt with blue stripes, a pair of khaki shorts and a towel that was beginning to turn black with dirt. In another corner was his green trunk with three red roses painted on it. Next to it were his boots, all ready to take off at a run. The odour of the crumpled red socks stuffed in the boots assailed my nostrils from time to time. Under the cot were empty coconut oil tins, an earthenware jar without a lid and slippers with a broken strap.

'Why do you keep empty tins under your cot, Kunhathu?' I asked.

'They'll be useful some day, child. Who knows when things like this will be needed? I never throw away anything. I pick up things that other people throw away. You can store rice and dal in these tins, can't you?'

I nodded. 'Yes,' I said.

'I'll take all these things when I go to Kottapadi on vacation.'

'You'll take Achan's broken slippers too?'

'Of course I will! Your father is a great man, child. My family stays alive thanks to his generosity. I'll keep his slippers in the prayer room, child. Let the children kiss them; they will be blessed by doing so. I'm going to place your father's slippers where St Joseph's picture is. If you rip open my heart, child, you'll see your father there. He's God, child. Do you know who he is?'

'Who is he?' I asked.

'That's a fine thing to ask! Doesn't anything I say get into your head? Haven't you heard the story of the person who asked what Sita was to Rama after listening to the entire *Ramayanam*? Your question is like that. As if I have to tell you who your father is! There's no one in the world who doesn't know who he is! Wasn't it your father who discovered the gas plant that was fixed to cars and lorries when the war caused a shortage of petrol? If a gas plant is tied to the back of a car, there's no need for petrol. He should be given the Veerashrinkhala award just for this discovery, child. In the old days, kings used to award the Veerashrinkhala to music composers and soldiers. It's a chain made with twenty-eight gold sovereigns—so heavy you can hardly lift it.'

'Do you have a Veerashrinkhala, Kunhathu?'

'Who would give this Kunhathu a Veerashrinkhala, child? There's no one in the world to buy me even a beedi stub. When I asked that man for a beedi the other day, he made a face at me like a monkey.'

'Who?'

'I won't mention names. I don't want anyone to get into trouble because of me. I want to live without quarrelling with anyone. I never poke my nose into anyone's business. And I don't want anyone to poke his nose into mine. That's all that really matters to me—do you understand that, child?'

I nodded.

'It's thanks to you, child, that I'm not bored. I need to talk to someone; otherwise I'd feel suffocated. We're all human beings, after all. We're bound to have sorrows locked up in us. If we don't speak of them to someone, we would suffocate and die. Haven't you heard of Dr P.B. Menon in Calicut? I used to work for him. He used to say it's good to weep; if you keep your sorrows inside you and don't weep, you'll have heart failure.'

'What's heart failure?' I asked.

'You know, don't you, child, that there's no one who doesn't have a heart? The heart is a rounded thing like a ball. A bright red ball. All our thoughts are inside it. Have you seen steam? Thoughts are like steam filling the ball. When it can't hold any more, the ball bursts—dhum! The heart breaks loudly, as loud as a cracker, the kind you throw into the air. An uncle of my wife's was a patient at the Calicut General Hospital. He had had surgery for piles. He was there for two days and I kept him company. While I was there, I heard the sound a heart makes when it breaks. Dhum: just like a cracker going off! God, how I trembled! It was a patient dying in the ward next to ours. The ball that was his heart burst suddenly. How everyone there wailed! His wife and children: all of them beat their chests

and wept. My wife's uncle said, "Take me home soon."
He was frightened. What if his heart burst too? Ha, ha!'

'Is your heart ready to break, Kunhathu?'

'I think it'll take a little more time; it'll break only after
everyone else's breaks. It's my wife that I'm afraid for.
She weeps and wails all the time. She weeps if the children
fail; she weeps if they pass! When Cheruchi passed her
exams, her mother cried. She said she wept for joy. She
weeps so much that she's become very thin and weak!
Your breath would blow her away. She's grown sunburnt
too. Do you know what she was like before she had my
children? Sleek as a poovan banana, with a skin like gold.
Yes, my wife was the colour of gold! Now she has
consumption. She wakes up at night and starts to cough.
And then? She doesn't spit out the phlegm. It chokes her,
lying heavily on her chest like a stone. Chakunni Doctor
told me the phlegm has no way of coming out. An
operation on her lungs might save her. But she might stop
breathing during the operation. The doctor's asked us to
take a decision. The phlegm might come out if we have
the operation done, but she could die. That's all. I said,
"No, Doctor, I'll be content to see her alive like this. Let
her cough day and night. I don't mind. At least the kids
have a mother to call out to. That's all I want. Don't
operate on her lungs."'

'What about her phlegm then?'

'Let it stay there. All she'll do is cough, isn't it? Let her
cough. Let those who don't want to listen to her cough
put their fingers in their ears. Ha, ha!'

'And what if your wife dies, Kunhathu?'

'Let her die then. Once you're born, you have to die,
don't you? I've put by the money to go as soon as the telegram
arrives. Don't tell anyone, child. I've kept it wrapped up

in a piece of paper in that green trunk there. All of a hundred rupees. If those wretches here—you know who I'm talking about, don't you?—come to know, they'll break open my trunk and steal the money. Inform me when the telegram comes. If I'm at work, you must telephone me. If you say PK one-six-two-o, you'll get through at once. Then you must say, "I want C.K. Mathews." Don't say "peon" or anything like that. Everyone knows me well. I take tea to everyone, child. So they're all fond of me. Ask that Kali Babu about me. He's sure to say, C.K. Mathews, very good man. Then K.S. Menon: he thinks the world of me. If he doesn't see me for just half an hour, he makes a racket. Menon is having a wooden doll's house made for you, child. He said it would be ready for your birthday. You should see how pretty it is! Four rooms, with chairs and tables, sofas and almirahs in them. Don't tell anyone I told you. You're so lucky, child! It's a secret, remember . . .'

❖

Once while my brother was doing geography lessons with Pot-Belly Master, I went to the classroom determined to do something to earn compliments from my wily companions.

My friends Saroja, Viswanath, Hiran (whom we called Bachu) and Santhu Banerjee waited hidden behind the door.

'Sir, you told us that the world revolves on an axis. Which country is that axis situated in? Which city? Which street?' I asked.

Master's dark face became the colour of a purple jamoon. The veins on his neck stood out. His eyes widened and the reddish nerves in them reminded me of a river outlined on a map.

'So you want to know where the axis of the world is, do you?' asked Master, grinding his false teeth. I saw the saliva frothing at the corners of his mouth and the trembling of his fingers.

'Yes, Sir, I want to know where the world's axis is situated.'

'Right here!' roared Master. The walking stick hanging behind the chair clattered to the ground. Neither Master nor I bothered to put it back in its place.

'Sir, do you mean the axis is here in this room?' I asked.

'Yes, in this room—on that chair!'

They must have heard his loud voice, for everyone came rushing from the kitchen and elsewhere.

I glanced at the door. I could see my companions' faces like half-moons behind it. Mustering courage, I turned to Master, 'Sir, you want us to believe that the world's axis is situated on this chair, don't you? In that case, you must be that axis yourself, isn't that so?' I asked.

'Yes, I myself am the world's axis,' he said.

My younger brother, who had been looking distressed, became tearful.

'Thank you for telling me this,' I said. My friends and the servants followed me silently as I went out. 'I hope you're all convinced now that Pot-Belly Master is mad! I've told you so many times . . .' I said.

This happened many years ago. I was certain then that Master was not right in his head. I realized later that what he had said was the truth. Each person is the axis of his own world. And no one else can control the speed at which that world spins around. Each of us creates an imaginary world right next to the real world. I learned that the energy one gathered from the real world could be put to use in the imaginary one and that from the imaginary world in the real one. The strength one draws from the imaginary world can be compared to the force gathered from a shadow. But in 1944, in the Lansdowne Road house where we lived, I thought mistakenly that Mr Francis Sequeira was mentally deranged.

Kunhathu hated Master. It infuriated him that Master got the bottles of alcohol which Achan's friends gave him at Christmas time by flattering Achan and talking sweetly to him. Which is why he would always ask me, 'Why not send this Pot-Belly away and appoint a woman teacher? What's the use of being educated? He is an ungrateful creature. He shouts at the child of the patron who pays him! He's not paid forty rupees a month to shout at the children!'

Kunhathu inhaled the pinch of snuff in his palm and raised his rheumy eyes to mine.

'Maybe I don't have a black coat and trousers,' he intoned in his dry voice, 'but I am grateful to those whom I serve. I am loyal to this family. If I have to give my life for them, I will . . . If you bring all kinds of people into the house and welcome them as teachers, they'll soon begin to think they're as important as their employers. You have to know your own place. Do you know that, child?'

I shook my head. 'No,' I said.

'What happened?' asked Kallu. 'Why did Pot-Belly Master scold the child? What did the child do?'

'I didn't do anything,' I said. Full of affection, Kallu gathered my dishevelled hair and bound it.

'I didn't do a thing. But everyone enjoys scolding me,' I said.

'That's the fate of the middle child: to be scolded. The eldest one is never scolded. It's the firstborn, after all! And no one wants to scold the youngest. But everyone finds fault with the middle one. It is my fate as well. I have two

elder sisters and two younger ones. So no one wants me.
No matter whose fault it is, I'm the one who is scolded.
How much I've wept! Devi, let me be born the eldest in
my next life! I ask for nothing else!' Kallu raised both her
hands to the sky, her eyes full of tears. Partaking of her
sorrow, I wept with her.

'Kallu Amma, don't make the child cry. She's the kind
that can't bear to see tears. You've made her sob now,
waving your hands and weeping like that!' Kunhathu
was angry.

'I remembered my misfortunes. I can't help thinking of
them now and then . . .' said Kallu.

'I don't think you've any reason to feel so sad. Who
enjoys so many good things as you do, Kallu Amma? Rice
with vegetables, meat and fish, all kinds of snacks, tea,
coffee, milk, buttermilk at regular intervals; different kinds
of oil for your hair and your body; the tonics Balamani
Amma buys you for improving your health. All the clothes
you need; gold for your neck and ears, and no meagre
quantity. The ear studs are a sovereign each and the chain
a solid two sovereigns. Silver anklets for your feet. If you
tell people about your sorrows, Kallu Amma, they'll laugh
at you! If no one has heard me, God will!' Kunhathu looked
at me, winked and laughed.

'Kallu is right,' I said. 'No one cares for a middle child.
That must be why Achan and Amma don't like me.'

'They like you all right. They don't know how to show
that they do, that's all. That's the way they're made,' said
Kunhathu.

'Don't you show your children that you love them,
Kunhathu?' I asked.

'Where do I have the time to show affection or grin
like a monkey, child? I go home to my village once every

two years. It's true I take them lengths of cloth to make shirts and frocks and all that. But I don't have the time to sit down and talk to them. I have to go and see all my relatives in Kottapadi, child. By the time I've seen them all, my leave is over and I have to get back to Calcutta. What can I say, child—before I feel I've seen the children properly, I have to come back! I've left my home and family and come here to put up with these Bengalis, all for sixty rupees a month.'

'You're lucky though. You're so stingy that you spend very little and you've put by enough money. I don't save a thing!' said Kallu.

'It's because I'm so careful that I'm able to put a little money into the post office. Would I be able to send money to Kottapadi if I wasn't stingy? A whole family in Kottapadi lives on my salary. If I spend all my money and have a good time, the six of them would starve to death. It's not that I don't know how to enjoy myself, Kallu Amma! I don't have that hard a heart,' said Kunhathu.

'I'm sure you wish you could drink, like Master,' said Kallu.

'Oh yes, Kallu, I could do with a drink sometimes. When I see that devil fawn over our Master and snatch all those whisky bottles, my heart breaks. But what can I do? I can't speak flattering words in English like he can.'

'He's mad,' said Kallu. 'When he talks to our little Sundaran, it sounds as if there's thunder rolling through the room! It's because that child is so soft-spoken that he doesn't say a thing. He's the gentlest of them all. You can place your finger in his mouth and he won't bite it!'

That night, before I went to bed, I complained to Amma about Pot-Belly Master. I told her it would be better to dismiss the man and appoint a woman instead.

'What do you have against him, Aami?' asked Amma.

'He doesn't like me,' I said.

'And why should you be upset if he doesn't like you?' asked Amma.

'I don't want anyone who doesn't like me to come to this house,' I said.

'He's harmless, and they don't have money. If Achan dismisses him, he and his wife will starve,' said Amma.

'Don't dismiss him then. I'll go away. I'll go to Nalapat,' I said. Amma laughed. I had thought my decision would sadden her.

Anyway, Achan told Master not to scold me and hurt my feelings.

'I don't want to hurt Kamala in any way,' said Master. 'Kamala comes in every now and then while I'm teaching Shyamsundar and asks me questions. And they're usually silly questions.'

'If you want any information, ask Appu,' Achan said to me.

Appu Ettan worked in the Indian branch of the American firm General Motors and he stayed in our house in a room on the south-east side on the ground floor.

'Is Pot-Belly Master the axis of the world?' I asked Appu Ettan.

'Who told you this?' asked Appu Ettan, rubbing lime paste on a betel leaf.

'Master said so himself.'

Appu Ettan sneezed three times, very loudly. Then he wiped his face hard with the cloth on his shoulder.

'I think it's time to send Pot-Belly Master to Kuthiravattom,' said Appu Ettan gravely.

'Where is Kuthiravattom?' I asked.

'Near Calicut.'

'What's special about it?' I asked.

'He'll find his own kind there.'

'Anglo-Indians?'

'Anglo-Indians, Nairs, Thiyas, Mapillas, Vettuvas: you'll find all of them at Kuthiravattom. They have singing and dancing there, and plays and the circus. It's great fun!'

'I want to go there too,' I said.

'You have to be a little bigger, Aami. I'll take you to Kuthiravattom then, I promise. Right?'

I nodded. Kunhathu coughed noisily, trying to suppress a laugh.

I realized only later that Kuthiravattom was a mental asylum.

❖

In the days when we stayed in Calcutta, my poet mother took no part whatsoever in the running of the house. Achan called my mother 'child'. He thought of her as a child as well. Amma did not have the freedom to enter the kitchen or do any housework. Achan believed that danger lurked in the kitchen in the form of fire, knives, chilli powder and boiling water. Therefore the running of the household was entrusted to our manager, Narayanan Nair. Narayanan Nair had a long-standing and firm relationship with the members of our family. We children respectfully called him 'Nanana' and were afraid of his temper.

Nanana always wore white. The most important task of his day was reading the newspaper, which is to say the Malayalam newspaper *Mathrubhumi*. Exactly at eleven in the morning, he would open the big door facing the road, spread an old towel on one of the steps at the entrance and get ready to read the paper. As he read, he would look from time to time towards us children playing among the flowerpots placed between the gate and the house and at the vehicles speeding down the road. When he caught sight of a car that he recognized, he would call out and tell us who its owner was.

He shouted as the Darbhanga Maharaja's Rolls Royce passed the gate, 'There goes the Darbhanga Maharaja's car!'

I said someone was in the back seat, leaning back with his eyes closed. 'I didn't see him properly. Was he wearing a crown?' I asked.

Narayanan Nair laughed contemptuously.

'The only king who wears a crown now is the British king, George VI. What crowns do our kings have? Aren't they all defeated monarchs?'

'If he doesn't have a crown, how did you know, Nanana, that he's a maharaja?'

'The Darbhanga Maharaja owns the largest number of shares in your father's company. I've seen him so many times. I've often seen the car at Walfords too. He bought it there. You can see cars like this if you go to your father's office, child. Only kings can buy them. Everyone wants to buy one, but it's not enough to want to, is it? You have to have the money. Do you know how much it costs, child? A lakh and a half!'

I asked excitedly, 'If you were to get a lakh and a half, Nanana, you'd buy a Rolls Royce, wouldn't you?'

'I'd never buy a car—not even if I had ten lakhs! If I had money, I'd start a hotel here in Calcutta. There's not a single hotel here where you get our kind of food. Nair bachelors find life very difficult. They can't stomach what the Bengalis eat, and they don't have the money to buy what the white men eat. I tell you, Calcutta is a hell for Nairs, child. The other day, our Pallyath Balan Nair said Bengalis add sugar even to fish curry! What can one do?

As your Appu Ettan says, you have to fill your stomach somehow, at least to keep your soul safe in its cage! You can't die when you want to, can you? Do you realize, child, why people arrive one by one here every Sunday afternoon, baring their teeth in a grin?'

I shook my head, 'No.'

'They don't come every Sunday out of love. It's because they know what kind of lunch we serve here. And once they eat here, they never forget the flavour of the food. Our food suits anyone's palate. Soup, cutlets, chappatis, rice. Malayali vegetable preparations like kalan and eriserry. Sambhar specially made for your mother. Pappadams and pickles. Salad, pudding, bananas, oranges and grapes. What more do they want? Which hotel has a menu like that? That's why I say we should have a hotel, here on Park Street or on Elgin Road, where Nairs and people of higher castes can eat.'

'How much money do you need to start a hotel?' I asked.

Narayanan Nair took off his glasses and put them in his pocket. He bit his upper lip, frowned and sat silent for a while. Maybe because he was deep in thought, his forehead with thick eyebrows seemed to grow darker.

'How much money do you need, Nanana, to start a hotel?' I asked.

'At least five thousand,' he said.

'Is that all?'

'For a hotel of a modest kind, yes. If your father likes the idea, child, it's not a difficult thing at all. But I won't ask him myself. He should really think of it himself. He helps so many others. But he's forgotten me. Remember when those women came here the other day? From the Kerala Mahila Samajam? Greedy creatures! No sooner had they asked than he gave them your ping-pong table

without even asking you! Why did you just look on silently?
You could have cried loudly. All these greedy creatures
come here, put on an act and take away everything. Your
mother doesn't say a thing; nor do you. And I don't have
the authority to obstruct anyone.'

My eyes suddenly filled with tears when I thought of
the table those Mahila Samajam members had taken away.

'The women who come here are practised in coquetry
and wiles. That's how they've learned how to collect things,
going from house to house. You have to be smart if you're
a woman. What's the point of being like your mother? A
woman's got to have the ability to keep aside the money
her husband earns with his hard work. Otherwise, in the
end, she'll have nothing. And not even a dog will look at
her if she doesn't have money.'

'Doesn't my mother know how to be coquettish?'

'No, she doesn't. And she'll never learn either. Women
born in good families don't know things like that, child.
Isn't your mother from a great taravad? She'll never be
able to act coquettish, not if she spends a lifetime trying.'

Narayanan Nair smiled. I was distressed. I was afraid
my mother would be reduced to dire poverty in the end.

'Amma received nine rupees yesterday for a poem she
sent,' I said.

'Nine rupees! Suppose your mother writes ten poems a
year. She'll get ninety rupees. If she writes continuously
for ten years, she'll get nine hundred rupees! And what's
the use of that? Even to open a tea shop you need a
thousand rupees. Suppose something happens to your
father. After all, he's a human being, isn't he? We have no
idea when God will call each of us to his abode above.
What if your father dies? What is your mother going to
do? She has to eat twice a day, after all; drink a couple of

cups of tea. She needs clothes and oil. She has to give the servants their salaries. What is she going to do? You have to be smart. If you're a woman, you should get hold of at least the money your husband earns. I'm not saying you have to put it in a bank. You can put it in a packet, slip the packet into your pillow and stitch up the edges. It will be under your head when you sleep. You can open it up when you want. To buy land. Or a house in Calcutta.'

I nodded. Kunhathu, who had been listening to Narayanan Nair while he was watering the plants, came up to me.

Smiling, he asked, 'Do you want to be rich, child?'

'No,' I said.

'So then? Your speech was a waste. The child belongs to Nalapat—don't forget that. No one in that family is besotted with money. The doctor said to me, if Appunni Menon wants to get married, he can find a Nalapat girl. Then I said, "Master, the girls in that family don't care about money. Girls from other families don't even allow their husbands to sleep peacefully—they ask for money all the time!" Isn't that right? I went to Thendiyath last time I went home on leave. They gave me five rupees and a mundu.'

'Who?' asked Nanana.

'Ammini Amma. Nalapat Ammini Amma. Who else would give me five rupees and a mundu?'

❖

'Shall I put a few drops of thanneerkudam in your eyes, Kamala?' asked Janaki, my schoolmate in Punnayoorkulam. The juice of the thanneerkudam was considered a good remedy for poor vision. Janaki held a sprig that resembled crabgrass in her hand. A dewdrop glistened on its tip.

'See this drop of liquid—that's a thanneerkudam,' said Janaki. 'A drop in your eye will sharpen your vision. My mother puts it in my eyes from time to time. That's why my vision is so good.'

I looked into her eyes. I liked the ashen colour of her pupils. 'Maybe I have light eyes,' she said, 'but they're really sharp. While I'm sitting in class, I can see the squirrel perched on top of the banana palm in Ayyappu's compound sipping honey from a flower. If you crush a nandyarvattom flower in your hand and let the juice drip into your eyes, that's excellent for your vision too. I'll do that for you. I want you to have sharp eyes like me. Then you can look at the squirrel sipping honey from the banana flower on Ayyappu's palm.'

The northern boundary of the school was a canal. During the monsoons, a river the colour of milky tea frothed and foamed along the canal. By the end of the monsoon, it would gradually be transformed into a thin rivulet. And streaks of black and pale red would suddenly run through the sand, changing its colour. We used to gather handfuls of sand as pale pink as a seashell to carry home. Wild grass of all kinds grew plentifully on the sides of the canal, medicinal herbs thriving amid weeds. I used to walk through the compound with Ammamma in the month of Karkatakam to learn from her how to distinguish the medicinal plants from the ordinary ones.

From the first of Karkatakam to the last day of the month, the traditional offerings that would attract Sri Bhagavathi to the house and bring good fortune to us would be displayed on a low, tortoise-shaped wooden stool placed in front of the machu, the household shrine: the ten sacred flowers, some sandalwood paste, a mirror of polished brass, sindooram and water in a bell-metal pot that had a spout. As soon as I had a bath, I would place a tilakam on my forehead with a paste made out of crushed mukutti flowers. Devaki always said that a mukutti flower with four petals would bring us good fortune and she and I used to spend hours wandering over the yard, searching . . .

'Shall I touch this to your eyes?' Janaki demanded impatiently.

'No.'

'Then you don't want your eyes to be sharp? If your vision isn't good, you could fall into the well or tread on a poisonous snake. The snake doesn't bother who its victim is—it just strikes. We'll have to send for the vaidyan to get rid of the poison. And he may well have gone to Kashi. So the poison will get into your body and you'll die. You want to die, don't you?'

'I don't want to die.'

'Then don't waste my time. Open your eyes. I'll let the thanneerkudam drip into your eyes.'

I turned my face away and ran through the canal. My feet sank into the wet sand and it felt as if snakes were reaching out to swallow them. I arrived at the steps leading up to school and waited for a minute, my heart beating fast.

Janaki stood far away, clutching the sprig of thanneerkudam in her hand. She wore a white skirt and a blouse with purple stripes. Her eyes glittered in the faint light.

I climbed up the steps. The peanut vendor sitting under the banyan tree smiled at me. Peanuts and a few pods of green tamarind were arranged on a tray before him.

'Do you want a piece of green tamarind?' he asked.

I shook my head to say no.

'Why are you out of breath, child? Did a buffalo chase you through the canal?'

'No.'

'Eat some peanuts. It doesn't matter if you don't have money.'

'I don't want any.'

When I could not see Janaki any longer, I ran to my classroom. A piece of iron taken out of a railway track was suspended from the ceiling on the northern verandah and Ayyappu was beating on it with a stick. The headmaster peered at his watch twice and entered class seven.

'Tell me the truth, child,' said Janaki. 'You hate me, don't you? It's Kottayath Thangam you like, isn't it?'

I did not bother to reply. Moideen, who usually sat on the same bench as I did, was not present. Thangam told me that he had typhoid. Appunni interrupted, saying he had died and Thachu Master, who had just come in to teach us arithmetic, was very angry.

'Is it to spread such rumours that you come to school?' he asked, cane in hand.

No one said a word about Moideen after that.

In the evening, Malathikutty said, 'Two people died of typhoid at home years and years ago: Cheria Oppu's children.'

We called Ammayi's elder sister Cheria Oppu. It was Meenakshi Edathi who had told Malathikutty that Cheria Oppu's two beautiful daughters had died one after the other of typhoid. They had been eighteen and seventeen. The elder one had gone to the temple in the morning and had come back complaining of a headache. She had died three days later. They had brought ice all the way from Kunnamkulam to bring the fever down but it had been of no use. The fever had kept rising.

Malathikutty and I once opened the steel trunk in which her clothes were kept and examined a silk blouse admiringly. It had frills at the neck and around the sleeve. Two of Malathikutty's uncles had gone to England to study. That must have been why the girls at Ambazhathel wore clothes like those of English women.

The blouse we found was bright pink. I tried it on and it came up to my knees!

'She was such a pretty girl!' said Meenakshi Edathi. 'Someone must have cast an evil eye on her. All this talk about typhoid is a lie. It was the evil eye that killed the child. There are lots of people in this village with the evil eye. One look from them and a whole mango or jackfruit tree can wither away! When she went to the temple that day, Thangakutty wore this pink blouse and a mundu with a gold border. She had worn a kuzhiminni necklace and had kajal in her eyes . . . how beautiful she looked. I was afraid when I looked at her that someone would cast an evil eye on her. And as soon as she came back, she fell ill . . .'

Malathikutty and I talked to each other about typhoid and the evil eye with fear in our hearts. I was terrified when I heard that flies carried typhoid germs. Flies buzzed all the time through the outhouse at Nalapat and the western room where they made tea. I thought the humming of their wings sounded like the hiss of death . . .

The questions I kept asking Ammamma about death distressed her. To make things worse, she was reading a book about the fear of death.

'Won't you be able to see me after you die, Ammamma?' I asked.

'The world of the dead is far away, isn't it? I might not be able to see you from there . . .' she answered.

'What if your eyes are very sharp?'

'Maybe I will, then,' she said.

I went with Janaki to the canal next day.

'I want some thanneerkudam,' I said.

'Oh, so you want to improve your vision now, do you?'

'It's not for me. I want to give it to Ammamma.'

'For what?'

'So that she can see me even after she dies,' I told Janaki, lowering my voice. She laughed.

'Don't you know dead people are burned? Their eyes burn too, along with the rest of them. There's nothing left but bones.'

'Will they burn my Ammamma?'

'Of course they will! I'm very sure of that. Everyone is burned—everyone in this world. I've heard that Cherumans and Nayadis are buried. Everyone else is burned.'

'Will I be burned?'

'When you die, you'll be burned. You can't keep dead people in the house, can you? They stink. Don't you know even that, child? Doesn't a rat stink when it's dead? When we die, we stink just like dead rats do!'

'What if my Ammamma and I don't die?'

Not only Janaki but all the children there laughed when I said that.

'Are you two divine beings that you won't ever die?' asked Janaki.

'I don't know.' The children rolled on the ground, laughing. Mirth distorted their faces hideously.

When I went back home that evening, Ammamma asked, 'Have you been crying, Kamala? Your eyes are red.'

'Are we human beings or divine women?'

'We're human beings, Kamala. Why are you asking me this?'

'So that means we'll die?' I asked in a trembling voice. Ammamma nodded.

'Then it's no use having sharp eyes, is it? Once you die, Ammamma, you'll never be able to see me again, no matter how much you want to, will you?'

'I can't answer questions like that, Kamala, I'm not wise enough.' Ammamma wiped her eyes with a towel.

The Days before Yesterday

One day, at dusk, some women with a little girl came on a visit to Nalapat. The child's front teeth were rotten. I did not like the way she smiled at me, baring her gums. Ammamma ordered me to play with her. I took her upstairs to the western bedroom, facing the mango tree.

The only thing I had of my own in those days was a doll. Its golden hair was made of floss. I used to call it 'Mamma'. Mamma was the bride at every doll's wedding that occurred in Punnayoorkulam.

The little girl placed my doll on her lap. Then she pretended to nurse it at her breast. I did not like this at all.

'What is your name?' I asked the girl.

'Mother's golden girl,' she answered, rolling her eyes.

'I meant your real name,' I said with displeasure.

'My real name is Prema,' she said.

'Don't give it any more trouble now—let it go to sleep,' I said, pointing to the doll.

Prema would not put the doll down. Worse, she would not give it back to me even when it was time for her to go. When her mother tried to take it from her, she began to cry loudly.

'She's quite obstinate, isn't she?' asked Ammamma.

'Obstinate? I've never seen anyone as obstinate as she is. The girl needs to be whipped,' muttered Prema's mother.

Devaki lowered her voice and said to the crying girl, 'Don't take away this child's doll. She doesn't have other dolls to play with.'

My eyes filled with tears.

'Ai, ai, Kamala, you're crying? For the sake of a doll? Let Prema take it. You can write to your father and he'll send you a pretty doll,' said Ammamma.

'I want Mamma. I don't want a new doll,' I sobbed.

'Let go of the doll! I'll punish you when we get home. I'll burn your thigh with a red-hot ladle! Imagine being so pig-headed! We should never have brought this little wretch with us.'

'I won't give you the doll,' said Prema.

'Let her take it. I'll console Kamala,' said Ammamma. She drew me towards her, stroked my head and fondled me.

'Mamma is *my* doll,' I said.

'You're a good girl, aren't you, Kamala? Are good girls selfish like this? Give it to that child,' said Ammamma.

'Fine thing!' said Devaki. 'The doll the child's father sent her from Calcutta to play with! What can she do if you insist on her giving it away? If someone were to ask you, would you give your wealth away, Valiamma?'

'Will you be quiet, Devaki? No one spoke about wealth here. What we're talking about is a doll!' said Ammamma.

'What wealth does our child have except this doll? Don't you know she goes to sleep every night with the doll in her arms? She never puts it down for a minute and now you're telling her to give it away! They're not even related to us, are they? Don't you see, our child is crying? Even if you say so, I won't allow our child's doll to be snatched away like this. They can go to Kunnamkulam and buy a doll if they want to. Or they'll certainly get one at Thrissur.

All they have to do is pay for it. It isn't as if this child here has eight or ten of them—she just has this one. The year before last, her father spent a lot of money and sent it to her,' said Devaki. But Prema's grip only grew tighter. And as for the doll, it lay inert in her arms.

'That's enough, Devaki. Don't make a speech. It's I who say she must give Prema the doll. Kamala will give it to her. I know Kamala's nature,' said Ammamma.

'Maybe she will. Of course the child will listen to your words, Valiamma. But this is a terrible sin, Valiamma. How many days our child will have to wait to get a new doll! And when she does get one, will she grow so attached to it? Haven't you seen the way carries it around, saying, "Mamma, Mamma"?' asked Devaki.

'Devaki Amma is right,' said Prema's mother. 'It's not right for your child to give her doll away.' Seated astride her mother's hip, Prema quickly hid her face in her mother's sari. But she did not loosen her grip on the doll.

'Give her the doll!' roared Prema's mother.

Prema opened her mouth wide and began to cry.

'It's *my* doll,' she said.

'The doll belongs to this child here—I'm certain of that!'

Sankaran rushed in, perhaps because he heard the raised voices. 'What's the matter, Valiamma? Why is our child crying?' he asked.

'Nothing's the matter, Sankara. You can go back to the kitchen,' said Ammamma.

'I'll go back to the kitchen. The kitchen is what Sankaran is fated to occupy. And I know that. But I find it difficult to work when our child is crying. Her parents aren't here. They entrusted the child to us. When people turn up determined to make the child unhappy, they shouldn't think there's no one here to defend her. The master in Calcutta once said to me, "Sankara, you must look after my child." Tell me, little one, who made you cry? Even if it's the princess of Eliyangode who did that, I won't let her go unpunished!'

'Don't talk rubbish, Sankara,' said Ammamma.

Prema's mother said, 'We'd better leave. It will be pitch dark by the time we reach home. I'll have to heat some water and give the girl a bath. If I bathe her in cold water, she starts to cough and gets feverish. We give her medicine for the cough every day. We pound the leaves of the adalodakam plant, squeeze out the juice and force a teaspoon of it into her mouth. But it's done her no good at all. I'm thinking of asking Cheerakuzhi Achuthan Nair to take a look at her.'

'Do that. Her cough is sure to disappear. Achuthan Nair is excellent at treating children,' said Ammamma.

Prema began to scream. Devaki had somehow managed to take the doll away from her.

'It's our child's doll. Let it stay here,' said Devaki, smiling.

The child's hollering became unbearable. Her skin turned purple.

'Give it back, Devaki. Kamala doesn't mind. Why should you and Sankaran protest so much if Kamala doesn't?'

'Our child hasn't really consented in her heart, Valiamma. Can't you make out how upset she is, looking at her eyes?'

'I won't go without the doll,' screamed Prema. Jupiter had risen in the sky. Ammamma's eyes wandered to the ilanji tree in the snake shrine. I knew she was thinking of how late she was for her bath and prayers.

'Kamala, will you give it to her?' asked Ammamma. She took the doll and handed it to Prema. I saw Mamma smiling at me. All she knew was to smile, poor thing.

'Now you can stop crying and go home,' said Ammamma.

'I'll try and visit you next month. I love coming here. Prema loves it too.' Prema turned round at the gate and smiled. I didn't smile back.

'What happened now? They took away our child's only toy. What'll she do now?' wailed Devaki.

'I'll make you a cart. A cart with four wheels. Those smart folk made off with your doll, didn't they?'

'She's not going to lose anything because the doll's gone,' said Ammamma. 'The child will be ruined if you teach her to be selfish.'

'And isn't it a selfish child who finally got the doll for herself? Who took our child's doll away? The child who's selfish—not just selfish, Valiamma, she's cunning as well. That's how she collects things for herself. Our child here is going to be like you, Valiamma. She won't have a paisa of her own!' said Sankaran.

I was afraid that Ammamma would scold him. But Ammamma laughed as if it were a joke.

'You're right, Sankara. I don't have a paisa of my own. But I've never betrayed anyone; you can be sure of that. I feel good when I think of it,' said Ammamma. When I went to her bed at night, I thought of Mamma and felt like crying again.

'Mamma will think of me and cry,' I said.

'She's only a doll. She's not alive,' said Ammamma.

'But I'm human—I'm alive. I feel sad because I can't see Mamma,' I said.

'You shouldn't grow deeply attached to anything, Kamala. When you find you're growing too fond of something, you must control your feelings. Otherwise all you'll know is sorrow.'

'Don't you feel affection for me, Ammamma? Won't you feel sad if you send me off to another house?'

Ammamma looked into my eyes and lay in silence for a long time. Then she said, 'Yes, Kamala, I'll feel sad. I'll feel very sad if I can't see you.'

❖

'Our mookolachathan's here, child!' cried Devaki, waking me up from an afternoon siesta.

'Our mookolachathan? Who's that?' I asked, sitting up in bed.

'How strange! Don't you know the mookolachathan, child? He came here last year in the month of Makaram. You laughed so much, watching him fling his arms and legs around. Surely you remember? Get up and come downstairs—he's been waiting such a long time just to see you.'

'Did he say he wanted to see me?'

'Does he have to say so? He won't go away until he's seen you. He says you have to give him a mundu with your hands. The mookolachathan is not like the parayankaali whose black form is so frightening that you'll urinate when you see him! Our mookolachathan is not like that at all: he's a gentle creature, kind and gentle!'

I heard a feeble drumming from the southern yard. I hurried down the stairs and ran to the patio.

His forehead and nose hidden behind a mask made of palm leaves, the mookolachathan was spinning over the sand, fluttering the palm-leaf wings attached to his legs. His feet crushed the kanhira flowers scattered over the yard. He turned to me and said something in a language I could not understand.

'What did he say?' I asked.

'You don't follow what he says, do you?' asked Devaki.

'What language is he speaking?' I asked.

'The language of the evil spirits,' said Sankaran. 'Do you know who they are? I don't think you've seen the residence of the Kattumadom Namboodiris. It's a fascinating place—you should see it. There's a temple there that's filled with darkness. If you peer through its black bars, you can see a thousand tiny evil gnomes. No, not a thousand, ten thousand! Some are only a foot high. But the power each of them wields! I begin to shiver with terror the moment I see them. There's a rule that you can't peer in, but you won't be able to resist looking. I went there to have a mantra sealed in an amulet so that I could wear it on a string and be able to sleep peacefully and not have nightmares. I met the senior Namboodiri who was to write the mantra. He looked so frightening! With eyes like burning cinders! "What do you want," he demanded in a voice like thunder. I urinated at once, child. I was so terrified!'

'Where does the mookolachathan come from?' I broke in. Sankaran was unhappy that I had interrupted the flow of his oration. He turned and walked quickly to the kitchen.

'Why does the child want to know where the mookolachathan's from? Is she going to marry him?' he cried out loudly from the kitchen.

'God will curse you if you say such impudent things about the child!' Valli shouted back.

'Be quiet, both of you,' said Devaki. 'If Valiamma wakes up and comes down, she'll scold everyone. Let me give the mookolachathan some rice and paddy and send him away. He's been jumping around the yard for hours!'

Valli, who was Mambulli Krishnan's wife, moved closer to me.

'Do you know who the mookolachathan is? He is a Vettuvan dressed up as the mookolachathan. And the

Parayan who lives on the other side of the field, the one who has learned sorcery and black magic . . . it's he who dresses up as the parayankaali. That's why he stands at the gate. Parayas are not allowed to come beyond the gate.'

The mookolachathan said something to me. Then he spun his head round and round, just like you move a ladle fast in a pan when stirring the contents. I was afraid his false nose would fall off. Nobody paid attention to the dance he did in the courtyard.

'What did the mookolachathan say to me?' I asked.

Valli laughed, displaying her worn teeth stained red with betel.

'He said you must go to the temple festival in Pavittamkulangara. If Valia Thampuratti gives me permission, I'll take you there,' said Valli. 'The Pavittamkulangara Bhagavathi's temple is right behind the Ambazhathel compound. You can hardly call it a temple— there's a Bhagavathi idol there, under a tree.'

'She has great power,' said Unnimaya's older sister, Padmavathi.

Devaki gave the mookolachathan's attendants rice and paddy. The mookolachathan turned to go, muttering something to himself.

'He's very fond of the child,' said Devaki. 'Everyone who comes here loves this child.'

'When Sankaran Kammal teases her, I feel upset,' declared Valli.

Sankaran suddenly appeared at the door. 'What do you mean? That I tease the child? Why would Sankaran ever do that? You can cut open my heart with a knife and you'll find the child's picture right inside! She's the one I care about most in this whole village. Did you know that, Valli? This house wakes up only when the child arrives from

Calcutta. Otherwise it's as lifeless as a wet chicken. Absolutely silent. You can eat your fill and sleep all you want, that's all. Is that enough for human beings? Don't we need something to be happy about? This child is the only person who talks to me. No one else here has any time to talk to me—they're all so busy, and as preoccupied as deputy collectors!'

'Send for your wife then, to talk to you,' said Devaki.

'Everyone in the world knows I don't have a wife!'

'And whose fault is that? You didn't want to marry, did you? Maybe you don't have enough money to look after a wife,' said Devaki. She stood leaning against the pillar, running her fingers briskly through my hair.

'Stop kicking a corpse,' muttered Sankaran.

'Where's the corpse?' I asked.

'Here, child,' cried Sankaran, striking his chest dramatically. 'A corpse that belongs to the government, one that no one will come to claim!'

'But you're not dead, Sankara,' I said.

'I'm dead, child. Sankaran's dead. Who needs me? Who except you cares for me, child? When they want something done, Sankaran is there to do it. Once that is over, they spit Sankaran out like a chewed curry leaf!'

'I don't get what you mean,' said Devaki.

'Don't touch my hair,' I said, brushing her away.

'I thought there might be lice in it. It's months since you came here, but you don't have a single louse! Doesn't it feel good when I run my fingers through your hair? If you want, I'll hunt for a fat louse in my hair and transfer it to yours. Then it'll multiply. And Devaki will have something to do. I can run my fingers through your hair all the time, find fat lice and crush them between my nails,' said Devaki.

'The child doesn't want to have lice in her hair!' said Sankaran. 'I'll tell Valiamma what you said.'

'Tell her if you want. Tell tales if that's what you want. No one can change your nature, not in this birth anyway,' said Devaki.

'They're fighting like cats and dogs all the time!' said Valli, laughing.

'It's all a farce,' said Unnimaya.

Valli asked me, 'Don't you want to go to the Punnoorkkavu temple festival, Cheria Thampuratti?'

I corrected her, 'No, the Pavittamkulangara festival.'

'If Valia Thampuratti agrees, I'll take you,' she said.

'Veluthedathu Lakshmikutty's going with that girl of hers,' said Devaki.

'If Bala's going, I want to go too,' I said.

'If you're going, child, I'll come too,' said Sankaran.

Devaki asked angrily, 'And who'll make the snacks for evening tea then?'

'Whoever wants can make them! I'm tired of stoking the fire all day—fed up. I'm going to Calcutta. I'll have no future unless I go there,' declared Sankaran, gesturing wildly.

'Oh yes, you're sure to get an officer's post as soon as you get to Calcutta!' said Devaki.

'I won't get an officer's post. My mother didn't have the means to educate me. It's true, I was born into a poor family. We don't have a paisa. But does that mean our necks have to be cut off? People who have no money have to survive in this world too, Devaki Amma . . .'

Devaki's eyes filled with tears and seeing them Sankaran wiped his eyes. I too felt like crying. I sobbed, not knowing the reason for my tears.

Valli was irritated. 'The two of you have made the child cry now.'

'I'm going,' said Unnimaya. 'Valiamma will come down now. I don't want to be scolded.' She hurried towards the gate, broom in hand.

That afternoon, while Ammamma and all the others were asleep, I went to the Pavittamkulangara temple to watch the Vela festival. The stone idols beneath the banyan tree were decorated with red thechhi and hibiscus flowers. The pleasant fragrance of burnt-out wicks hung heavily in the air. I saw legless horses and bulls made of bamboo. There were men selling bangles and murukkus, and hawkers wandered around with lengths of dotted material draped over their shoulders. The village women who had gathered there, their thick, oiled hair full of flowers, gave me mocking smiles. Blind Kuttappan Bhagavathar and Pot-Belly Raman Nair were there.

'There's the bhagavathar!' cried out Bala eagerly.

'The girl won't move from here now. She's crazy about music. She can never hear enough of it. When I ask her to help me wash clothes, she goes away and hides! She's bone lazy. She pulls a long face if I just tell her to sweep the floor with a broom.' Lakshmikutty had her left arm around Bala, but she put on a pretence of being angry.

'She's young, after all. How old is she?'

'I delivered her the day before the cyclone. We thought our hut would collapse and stayed awake all night. And this girl here was a real handful. Wouldn't suckle at my breast. We mixed some honey with water and touched it to her tongue from time to time—that's how she survived. What was I saying? Yes, the day before the cyclone. Or the day before that. So she must be about five now. I wanted to have her horoscope drawn up, but I couldn't. Didn't have enough money. If you don't give the Pannikkar a whole rupee, he won't chart a lucky horoscope. After all, he has to make a living too, doesn't he?'

'There's a person who comes to the house, a Variar. He's called Shoolapani. You can give him the rupee. They say that all the horoscopes he draws up are excellent,' said Devaki.

'Let me know when he comes next.'

'It was he who wrote this child's horoscope. She'll follow seven paths of good fortune, they say! Those who have money can have all the good fortune they want in their destiny. What destiny do the poor have? Work, work, work till you die!' muttered Devaki.

'Destiny indeed! I sometimes think it's just a hoax. I was told that my horoscope has a most auspicious configuration of planets, what they call the kesariyogam. And what happened? Do I ever get a moment to sit down and relax? I boil clothes, wash them and dry them from morning to night, year in and year out. Don't even have anyone to help. When my girl grows up, I'll hand her over to some young man and let the two of them take over the washing. I'm not up to it any more. Look at my hands: is there any skin left on them? That's because I bleach the clothes with my hands. The moment I begin to bleach clothes, my hands start to burn . . . as if I've put them into a lime-kiln. They're all burnt. But I can't stop washing clothes, can I? We have to eat—I have to feed this girl, don't I?'

'What if your son-in-law says he can't be bothered to do the washing? What will you do then?' asked Devaki.

'My daughter's man will after all be a Veluthedan by caste, a washerman. I won't marry her off without being sure of that. Are there Veluthedans who don't like to wash clothes? If there are, I've never heard of them!' said Lakshmikutty.

'I want to marry the bhagavathar!' cried Bala loudly.

'Indeed! Kuttappan Bhagavathar is old enough to be your grandfather. What desires the child has!' said Lakshmikutty.

Kuttappan Bhagavathar tilted his head to one side and smiled into the empty air.

❖

'It's the Jnavanankattu festival today. They'll fill paras, wooden measures, with paddy and give them to the temple.' Devaki poured out water for me as she spoke.

The drums had already started beating in the distance. Carried on the wind, the drumbeats echoed past the northern field and the carpenters' shed like thunder reverberating through the air.

'It'll be noon by the time they get here,' said Devaki.

'There's not a festival procession that doesn't stop at Thendiyath,' said Padmavathi, who was sweeping the courtyard.

'Maybe they will go to Thendiyath,' said Devaki, 'but I know they will certainly go to Ambazhathel.'

'How many of them come here?' I asked.

'Just four of them—we stopped the rest. They're a lot of work, child. By the time they come, you have to lay a banana leaf with its pointed end facing left, with a measure of paddy and a sheaf of coconut flowers on top of it: it's an offering to God. People here don't really believe in all this. Do you see Valiamma go to the temple? She goes on this child's birthday, that's about it. Other people go to Govindapuram or Pavittamkulangara and spend hours in worship. Well, it's true you don't earn any money worshipping God!'

'Who are you talking about?' asked Padmavathi.

'No one in particular. I don't belong to this place and when I go to the temples around here, I don't feel any sense of devotion. I go along with Valiamma when she goes, that's all. My bhagavathi is the Mookkola Bhagavathi—no one has the power she has. So why should I go to the temples here?'

'You're just stubborn, that's what you are. The gods in this place are very powerful. Try making an offering to our Punnorkkavu Bhagavathi. She'll give you whatever you desire. Govindapuram is no less powerful. It's not right to find fault with gods.'

'Padmavathi, you're not allowed to enter the innermost shrine in Govindapuram, are you? Then how can you pretend to have such devotion?'

'How can I enter the innermost shrine? We're Chaliyas. You talk like a little child sometimes! How can you ignore caste and creed?'

'The God who created the Brahmin priest created Padmavathi as well. Then how can God be so partial?'

'You're crazy! I can't argue with you. There, the drums are coming nearer. Light the lamp quickly and keep it in front of the house.' To the left of the main hall there was a little stage. That was where we generally placed the lamp and the objects for the offering.

'They're very early today,' said Devaki, sounding displeased. Among the drummers in the Jnavanankattu procession, there was a velichappadu with curly hair and a flat bottom. Possessed by the rhythm of the drumbeats, he began to dance. His hair flying, he twirled his scimitar and took measured steps towards Ammaman. He was an oracle now, ready to pronounce his predictions. Ammaman grunted. The velichappadu turned to Ammamma and mumbled. She said, 'That's enough. That's fine.'

The velichappadu threw rice grains over my head. I moved towards Ammamma.

'Don't be afraid, child. The velichappadu is not just a dancer now—he's become Bhagavathi herself. Bhagavathi won't harm anyone,' whispered Devaki in my ear. As the dancing slowed down, the rhythm of the drums slackened. The velichappadu sat on the ground and drank water drawn from the well. A disciple unfastened his belt of brass bells and took his scimitar.

'Is he Bhagavathi now?' I asked.

'No, he isn't. He's just a velichappadu,' said Devaki, smiling. The velichappadu gathered his long hair in his left hand and looked at me. Ammamma gave me an eight-anna coin to give him.

There was not a single procession that didn't go to Ambazhathel. As soon as they arrived there, Ittiyachan or Meenakshi Edathi would come home to collect me. No velichappadu ever cut open his scalp in Nalapat. At Ambazhathel, many velichappadu dancers would gash their scalps with the scimitar and rub turmeric into the wound later to help it heal. When all the members of the large Ambazhathel family crowded into the courtyard, the velichappadus would begin to dance faster and faster and would rapidly became possessed. They would turn into oracles and proclaim their predictions loudly, dancing frenziedly in tune with the drums.

The oracle would speak first to the matriarch, Parukutty Amma, our Cheria Oppu. You had to stand close to understand the words.

'I'll take care of the children and see that they never fall ill. Is that not enough?' asked the velichappadu. Cheria Oppu nodded.

Kunhunni Ettan, who had been waiting, hoping to hear the oracle say something about the court case in Ponnani, went into the house.

'Did the velichappadu say you would win the case?' his wife asked. Kunhunni Ettan did not reply. He had strong rationalist views. He used to talk to the children with great enthusiasm about the progress of science.

'Can girls become velichappadus?' I asked Ammamma.

'Why, do you want to become one?'

I nodded.

'No, girls cannot dance like that. If you're born a girl, there are things you can never do. If you do the velichappadu dance, you can never have babies.'

'I don't have the slightest desire to produce babies,' I said.

'But don't you want children of your own, Kamala?'

'I don't like little children,' I said.

Ammamma and Devaki laughed.

'Why don't you like children, Kamala?' asked Ammamma.

'They'll break my dolls and damage all my toys. I don't want children!'

'All right, all right. You needn't have babies, Kamala. All you want are dolls, right?'

'Why are you talking such nonsense, child? When you've been married for a long time, won't your husband say, "I don't want this barren wife"? Do you want to be a machi, a woman who can't have children?'

I suddenly thought of my beautiful Ammayi, the wife of my mother's uncle Narayana Menon. An elegant woman who covered her body with jewels. She didn't have children.

'Is Kutti Oppu a machi?' I asked. Ammamma and Devaki were silent.

'If Kutti Oppu is a machi, I want to be a machi too. I want to be as beautiful as she is.'

'What a child, talking all the time about wanting to be beautiful! Don't you know it's God who gives people beauty? Can you buy a fair complexion, long hair and shapely limbs from a shop? There used to be an ancient belief that if you swept and cleaned the steps of the bathing tank after your bath, you would become more beautiful. That girls who made all the ritual offerings in the month of Karkatakam would grow graceful and good. And I know that if you get up before dawn during the Thiruvathira season, have a dip in the pond and climb on a swing, you'll really be beautiful. You must eat koova porridge as well— it's cool. And drink tender coconut water. That's how girls become beautiful . . .' said Devaki.

'Stay here, Kamala. If you go back to Calcutta, you'll grow darker than ever,' said Ammamma.

'Is my father dark-skinned because he lives in Calcutta?'

'I don't know about that.'

'And Ammaman is fair because he lives here!' I added.

'Maybe,' said Ammamma, laughing.

'Did he go on the swing every Thiruvathira season? And dance the Thiruvathirakkali?'

'No!'

'He's fair because he rubs pindathailam over his body every day before he has a bath. Maybe if we try rubbing some of it on this child, her skin will grow fairer. It might even grow all flushed like the Master's,' said Devaki.

Ammamma could not stop laughing at that.

❖

Malathikutty of Ambazhathel house had a silk frock: it was chocolate coloured with a pattern of palm fronds all over. It made me wildly envious. I described it to

Ammamma over and over again, telling her how pretty it was. I used to talk to Ammamma every night until I fell asleep, pouring out my heart to her.

'I want a silk frock too,' I said to her.

Ammamma ran her fingers through my hair. 'Write to your father in Calcutta, Kamala. He will buy you one.'

'Achan won't send me anything.'

'But you've never written to your father to send you a frock. How will he know you want a silk frock?'

'I have—I wrote many, many times. I wrote and asked him to send me a frock, a gold chain, dangling umbrella-earrings, anklets . . . He doesn't even reply.'

'He must be busy. He'll write to you when he has the time. And he'll send you a silk frock. He'll bring you everything you want when he comes for Onam.'

When Achan came home to Punnayoorkulam on leave during the Onam season, all he brought me was a huge tin of Huntley and Palmer biscuits. I was afraid my playmates would ridicule my father's lack of concern. So whenever anyone asked what my father had brought me from Calcutta, I would say firmly, 'He hasn't had time to open his suitcase.'

'Can't you open it yourself, Aami? So what if he's busy, you can do it . . .' urged the children.

'It's locked,' I said.

'The key must be under his pillow. Go and look!'

'I can't behave like a thief.'

'Do you think opening one's own father's suitcase is being like a thief? You're mad!'

Their mocking laughter wounded me intolerably.

I said to Ammamma, 'I won't go to school unless I have a silk frock.'

Ammamma realized the seriousness of the matter. She sent for Kumaran, the tailor. Kumaran was a short, young man who always wore white. He would listen to everything Ammamma said and grunt in reply. He would never speak.

'You have to buy some silk, Kumara, from somewhere. Kamala says she can't do without a silk frock.'

'It has to be red silk,' I said.

Kumaran grunted. Sankaran came out to the verandah and said to Kumaran, 'Look here, silk is very expensive. Don't cut it like you usually do and make a mess of it. The frock you made for her last Vishu looks like a mendicant's robe. If you can't sew properly, you should just say so, you oaf!'

Kumaran did not say anything, nor did he look at Sankaran.

I turned to Ammamma. 'What's a mendicant's robe?'

'Valiamma doesn't know,' said Sankaran. 'I'll tell you what it is. The frocks you wear are like gosai robes, child, garments that hang loose on you. Haven't you seen the frocks that child from Ambazhathel wears? They're so pretty. This silly fellow makes a mess of all your frocks, cutting them so large!'

'Go to the kitchen, Sankara. Ettan will come to have his tea now. I'll take care of the child's frock.'

'All right, Sankaran will go back to the kitchen. I have to grate some coconut. Master's nearly finished his bath . . .'

Sankaran continued to mutter to himself about my frock even after he had reached the kitchen. 'A little child like her! My heart breaks when I see her go to school wearing a gosai robe. Valiamma doesn't know what kind of frocks the other children wear. Does the Ambazhathel child ever wear a gosai robe? Never! That's why I say, our child will look so pretty if she wears a nice frock. It's not as if this oaf doesn't know how to sew—other children's frocks come out so well. He thinks this is enough for our child . . .'

'Make it a little smaller in size, Kumara,' said Ammamma.

'I must have a red silk frock,' I said.

'Will you go to Thrissur, Kumara? Or will you buy the silk in Kunnamkulam?' asked Ammamma.

Kumaran broke his long silence, 'You can buy silk in Kunnamkulam. A gold-coloured material with stripes. I bought some and took it to Dr Kumaran's house, the house on the beach. They liked it very much. They gave me the price I asked for. There's the doctor's daughter Ramani and his sister Devaki. I made skirts and blouses for both of them.'

'I don't want striped silk. I want red silk.'

'I thought you people here don't fancy silk. That's why I never brought any here. I thought this child wears only handspun or mill-made khadar. I thought everyone here belongs to the Congress party,' said Kumaran, a smile gleaming below his moustache.

'What does the child have to do with the Congress party? She's been wanting a silk frock for such a long time,' said Ammamma.

'What are you discussing here?' asked Achan, coming towards us.

'Kamala says she wants a silk frock. I thought I'd ask Kumaran to get the silk from Kunnamkulam,' said Ammamma.

'Aami wants a silk frock? Ai, ai, disgraceful! Whose child are you? You know your father and mother never wear silk. Learn from your mother—don't you know she wears only khadar saris? Have you ever seen her wear a silk sari? It's not good to be so crazy about clothes.'

'I want a red silk frock,' I said.

'A red silk frock? Are you going to play a king's role in a play or something? Che, what will people think if they see my daughter walking around in a red silk frock? I'll send you beautiful white frocks. White is the only colour that suits you. Only fair children can wear dark colours,' said Achan.

'Then I don't have to go to Thrissur,' muttered Kumaran.

'You don't. I'll send her frocks from Calcutta. She can't wear red. If she does, it's me people will laugh at. Aami, you must never be conspicuous. Only uncultured people are conspicuous in their dress and behaviour.'

'Then we don't need anything now,' said Ammamma.

I felt suffocated. I hugged Ammamma, concealing my tears.

'Why do you cling to Ammamma all the time? Come. Come and walk with me,' said Achan, dragging me by the hand.

Achan usually walked very fast, hitting his walking stick on the ground from time to time or twirling it in the air. I had to run to keep up with him. Dry punna seeds were scattered under the punna tree. When I stooped to pick them up, Achan scolded me.

'You've become an ill-behaved rustic,' he said. I realized with astonishment that my tears tasted of salt.

'You know the war has ended. I'll take you to Calcutta now. I'll send you to school there and make you a smart girl. If you stay with your grandmother, you'll turn into a villager. I don't like that. You must learn to speak with courage to everyone and never have an inferiority complex. You must remember you're better than everyone else. You're my daughter. Never forget that.'

I did not say anything. The children who were playing marbles in the carpenters' workshed stopped playing and looked at us. I felt very proud of my father's stature. He wore a white shirt and white trousers. He had a packet of Gold Flake in one pocket and a purse full of money in the other. He wore a khaki topee to protect himself against the sun. I was suddenly afraid my companions would laugh at it.

'It's not sunny now—you don't need a hat,' I said to him.

'You'll begin to feel the heat as you walk. It will be burning by the time we reach school.'

'Do you have to go to school?' I asked.

'Of course! I have to meet your teachers. Do you have a master or a woman to teach you?'

'We have both. I like Sukumaran Master the best. He teaches history. Indian history. I like the chapter on Nur Jehan. Do you know all about her?'

'The Mughal queen. You seem to be very fond of kings and queens.'

'Yes, I am. I want to be a queen.'

My father laughed aloud. Ipe, who rang the school bell, stared at us, then shook his head and hurried away. I wondered whether he had stared at us because of Achan's hat.

'No one wears a topee here,' I said.

'They don't?'

'No. They don't wear trousers either. They wear mundus. The children call those who wear hats and trousers "white sayibs".'

Achan laughed loudly again. I saw a man in a mundu and a black coat near the fence. With him was his son, a lanky boy.

'Father, will you buy me sweets?' the child kept asking plaintively.

'V.M. Nair, isn't it?' asked the man in the black coat. He had a walking stick in his hand.

'Yes,' said my father.

'I'm Komwon,' he said. He held forth for a long time about courts and lawyers. The boy performed gymnastics on the sand, probably hoping to impress me. He had buck teeth. When he grew tired of his feats, he started to pluck the seeds on the plants that grew near the fence. 'To get over my tiredness,' he said. He ate like a monkey, screwing up his eyes and grinning.

'Do you want to eat any?' he asked.

'I'm not feeling tired.'

'If you walk further in this heat, you will feel tired,' he said.

I smiled.

'Who's the hatted sayib? Your father?' he asked, pointing to Achan.

I didn't answer.

While returning, I asked Achan, 'Why is that man called Komwon? Is that an Englishman's name?'

Achan laughed. 'Did you think he was an Englishman, Aami? He must be Komu Menon. He must have shortened it to Komwon.'

'The boy is very rude,' I said.

'Why, didn't you like him?'

'He was performing all the time, as if to show me he's as clever as a circus performer.'

'Don't you like the circus, Aami?'

'I've never seen a real one. We saw a trapeze act once, with the Ambazhathel children. We stood in Balettan's shop and watched it.'

'I'll take you to a fine circus in Calcutta. It's not like a trapeze act in the villages. There'll be lions and elephants and clowns . . .'

'Won't we take Ammamma to Calcutta?'

'How can we take her? Doesn't she have to look after things here? She'll stay in the village. I'll take you with me and make you an elegant, fashionable girl. Right?'

At that moment, I dreaded the city and its fashionable ways, the circus, everything . . .

❖   •

My father's close friend, K.P.R. Menon, once brought us a huge black and gold tin full of sweets. When the sweets were over, Ettan started to hoard coins in the tin. From the time we could remember, my father used to give my brother and me silver coins whenever he wished to express happiness. We had weekly tests at St Cecilia's European School. If we scored high marks in a test, he would give us a one rupee coin each. Coins were made of pure silver in those days. I always spent my money without a thought for the future. Every day, I bought Nestlé's chocolate from the cigarette shop situated a furlong away from home and ice cream from the Magnolia ice cream man who went through the streets with a yellow box fixed to his bicycle. And I always gave my miser of a brother a share as well.

My brother did not abandon his box even when we moved to Kerala during the war. He would put away the money Ammaman, Ammayi and Ammamma gave him on Vishu day. He once told me he would open the box when it was full, buy a cannon suitable for war and fix it near the gate of Nalapat.

'Or else I'll buy a fighter plane. So that if the war comes here, Nalapat will be safe.'

When Achan came home on leave, he opened the box and counted the money in it. There was a sizeable sum. Achan laughed and congratulated Ettan. With that money

Achan bought the deserted piece of land called the blacksmith's compound, in Amma's name. An acre of swampy land. It lay to the west of Nalapat. When it became part of Nalapat, it was our servants who rejoiced the most. They would go at twilight into the thick bushes that grew there to defecate in privacy.

Ettan stopped hoarding coins from that time.

Kunhunni Raja, my mother's father, belonged to the Chittanjoor kovilakam. He died of high blood pressure a year before I was born. The Chittanjoor kovilakam stood next to the Manikanteswaram temple. Called Madappattu, it was a beautiful area with five snake shrines on it. A paradise that spread over five and a half acres. The kovilakam had been built in the modern style, with glass panes.

One evening my family took me to the Chittanjoor kovilakam. I met a young girl there who suffered from a heart ailment, seated beside piles of books, twiddling the knobs of a radio. She must have been about fourteen. I saw a wonderful radiance on her face. Her thick hair was a perfect frame for the pale face. Only her lips were dark. She smiled at me but did not speak.

On our way back to Nalapat, our group talked unceasingly about the seriousness of that girl's illness.

'What is her name?' I asked.

'Sharada Thambatti,' said Marath Chinnu Amma. 'Her brother studies in Madras. He sent her that radio to help her pass the time. She twists and turns the knobs all day, listening to songs and speeches. Poor thing!'

'The brother's name is Unni Raja.'

'Everyone dotes on her.'

When Sharada Thambatti died, the family sold the kovilakam and the grounds to my father and moved to a town. My newly rich father was not interested in maintaining that beautiful palace. In five months it was demolished and its gigantic beams and doors, the broad granite steps of its tank, the long spouts shaped like gargoyles' heads that drained the water from the indoor toilets were all thrown into the western yard of Nalapat. Achan sent for carpenters and masons from various places to build an elegant mansion for Amma in the blacksmith's compound.

Cheriamma, my mother's younger sister, inherited the Chittanjoor Raja's flared nostrils and thick eyebrows. Amma and Cheriamma received an ample share of the royal family's keen intelligence. Amma could not have been the scholar she became merely because she was born in Nalapat. Her special flair for argument and debate was certainly not inherited from her mother's family.

Once when my father came home to Kerala on holiday, he called us to him and said, 'You can think up whatever mischievous pranks you want. But you must never give your mother any trouble. If you do, I'll thrash you.'

We never understood why Achan gave us this warning. Anyway, from that moment, we began to talk to Amma less and less, anxious not to give her trouble. We turned to Ammaman to clear our doubts. And to Ammamma for affection. It was common practice then to scold or thrash children. I had often heard our relatives threaten their children, 'I'll kill you . . . I'll break your legs.' No one ever spoke that way at Nalapat. Ammaman had studied child psychology. He tried to inculcate self-confidence in us by heaping praise on us, encouraging us in everything we did.

Ettan, who was only ten years old at the time, started a magazine and was its editor. We called it *Suprabhatham*. You could count the publications of that period on the fingers of your hand. We got some of them like

Mathrubhumi, *Manorama*, *Mangalodayam* and *Parijatham* at Nalapat. We had numerous stories, poems, essays and cartoons in our magazine. Many appreciative readers came to Nalapat to borrow copies of *Suprabhatham*. When Joseph Mundasserry came to Nalapat once, Ammaman gave him a copy of the magazine.

Mundasserry wore an ochre-coloured khadi shirt and a khadi mundu with a green border. His hair was greying, but thick.

His face was copper coloured. My brother worshipped Mundasserry and tried to copy his harsh style of critical writing. There were people who thought that the critical essays my brother wrote in *Suprabhatham* under the pen-name Shakarji were written by Mundasserry Master. But only people like my Ammamma really believed that Joseph Mundasserry would send articles every month to a ten-year-old editor! Ammamma was like that: she believed everything she was told. When I told Ammamma that the British royal family came to Calcutta and visited our school, she believed that too. I burned in the fires of repentance for three days before I told Ammamma the truth.

'I said it for fun. The British king and his children did not come to Calcutta at all. I just made it up.'

'But you never tell lies, Kamala. You must have dreamt it.'

While we were in Calcutta, I declared once that I had seen Sri Krishnan, the gopikas and their cows. My parents thought at first that I was delirious with fever. Ettan and I used to sleep on either side of my mother in those days on a four-poster. One night, after everyone had fallen asleep, I heard the swish of a broom under the bed as if someone were sweeping the place. Gradually, the figure of a woman took shape. She was middle aged and wore a white sari. When she disappeared with the broom, I heard a door being opened. It was after that that the colourful procession began to walk along the room, close to the wall. Sri Krishnan was there and the gopikas and cows with bells around their necks. When I told Achan and Amma, they lighted a lamp to show me there was no one there. But the figures were still before me. I saw Sri Krishnan both while I was asleep and while I was awake. The whole thing happened again next morning at eleven.

'You were just bluffing, weren't you, Aami?' asked Achan.

'No, I wasn't. I saw Unni Krishnan clearly,' I said.

But although Sri Krishnan had appeared to me, there was no significant change in my life. No special radiance touched my face. I had the kind of appearance that no one turned back to look at twice. Ammamma was the only person who caressed me. I had value and stature only in her eyes.

One day Ammaman asked, 'Aami, Bala told me that you saw Sri Krishnan. How are you sure it was him? Did the face you saw look like the face in the picture hanging in the puja room in the western wing?'

'No, it was not the same face.'

'Then how did you know it was Sri Krishnan you saw?'

'I heard the sound of the bells around the cows' necks,' I said.

The next time the children laughed at me about this, Ammaman took my side and asked them, 'What proof have you that Aami did not see Sri Krishnan?'

The children had no answer to that.

Ammaman told me that people see in the external world only what they have in their hearts. If a person harboured ghosts and devils in his heart, he would see them before his eyes as well.

Once, when we were at Guruvayoor, Ammaman insisted that I go into the inner shrine. I hated touching strangers' bodies. I liked to see the obese bodies that were hoisted on to the scales outside to make an offering of bananas or jaggery that equalled their weight.

The disfigured people who jostled against each other at the shrine—devotees whom no one cared for—shouted, 'Krishna, Guruvayoorappa, protect us . . .'

'I don't want to see Sri Krishnan. I want to go out,' I said to Ammamma.

'Will Krishnan like it that you came so far and didn't wait to see him?' she asked. She had assumed that I was Sri Krishnan's special friend. After all, he had appeared in my room once.

'I don't want to see him,' I said, annoyed.

'Pray that you'll pass your exams, child,' said Devaki.

'I don't need anyone's help to pass the exam,' I said.

Ammamma told me that arrogance destroys people in the end. She told me a story about some foolish people who thought they were greater than God, repented later, performed rites of penance and attained redemption. This prompted Devaki to close her eyes tight, join her palms and call out loudly, 'My Guruvayoorappa, I've not done anything wrong. Don't test me, Guruvayoorappa!'

'Why is Devaki crying?' I asked. Two teardrops fell slowly from her eyes on to her cheeks.

'I'm not crying, child. Why should I cry? I've done nothing wrong. I wept with joy when I saw Guruvayoorappan. I am fortunate—I could see the image so clearly. Sometimes when I come here, the shrine is closed and I have to go back without seeing him. Then my heart fills with despair. But today everything went off so well. Did you see him, child? His body all smeared with sandalwood paste, decked

in jewels . . . how beautiful he looks! There's no ailment
that can't be cured if you stay in Guruvayoor for seven
days, worshipping Him. An old Namboodiri who had
leprosy once came here to worship the deity. Every morning
he used to immerse himself in the temple tank and attend
the first puja of the day. He would drink the theertham.
In the afternoon, he'd eat the rice that had been cooked as
an offering to the deity and sit by a pillar listening to the
Bhagavatham being read. And what happened? He was
cured! Completely cured, child. It's the verses he composed
that are still sung here today. If you don't believe me, child,
ask your grandmother.'

I asked Ammamma, 'Was the old Namboodiri's leprosy
cured?'

'Yes. He was completely cured. His name was
Melpathoor Bhattadirippad. Don't you know, it was he
who wrote the *Narayaneeyam?* Haven't you heard verses
from it, Kamala?'

'I don't remember,' I said.

From the temple, we went to Achan's house,
Vadekkara. My father's younger brother, who was seated
in front of the house, leaning against the pillar and chewing
betel leaves, recited a verse from the *Narayaneeyam* to
me. The one that starts *bahudvandena ratnojvala
valayabhrithashona panipravale . . .* I learned it from him.
When I went back home, I recited it to Muthassi.

'You must teach me that verse,' said Devaki.

But however hard she tried, she could not master it. I
abandoned my efforts to teach her in the end and taught
her another simple one instead.

Deivame kaithozham kanumarakanam
Pavamanennenee kakkumarakanam . . .

'This is a much nicer verse,' said Devaki. 'The other one's full of English words. I couldn't understand a thing!'

No matter how many times Ammamma explained to Devaki that the *Narayaneeyam* had no English words, that it was written in Sanskrit, she would not believe her! 'Valiamma's just telling stories! Devaki's not such a fool. The moment I hear English, I know it's English. Haven't I been hearing the English this child speaks for days?' Devaki would ask, smiling.

❖

The first novel I read as a child was *Chintamani*. Beautifully narrated, the old tale tells of how a good princess was imprisoned by her enemy in a cell right on top of a fortress and how she was freed by the efforts of a parrot. After reading that story I began to see birds and animals as my friends. I wanted to get hold of a parrot as my eternal companion.

'What can I do if you insist on having a parrot? I'll ask the gypsies for one when they come. If crows will do, I can catch them for you. There are huge crows that come and sit outside, where we wash the vessels. They like to watch me clean the rice. I'll catch a big one for you,' said Sankaran.

'I don't want a crow,' I said.

'Why, what does a crow lack? Maybe it's black. But hasn't it been said that there's beauty in black as well? Then, some crows are cross-eyed. So what? Don't people say it's lucky to be cross-eyed? There are so many cross-eyed people in this village—aren't they happy? All of them are rich. They have wealth, children, houses, chains, bangles . . . everything!' said Sankaran.

'I know who you're talking about,' said Devaki.

'Are you trying to tell me you can see what's lying deep in my heart?' asked Sankaran.

Devaki was grating coconut for chutney. She had had her bath early morning and had gone to the temple—I saw the sandalwood paste and the sindooram on her forehead. Her hair was bound at the tip and had a tulasi leaf and a sprig of thechhi tucked into it.

'Did you go to the temple, Devaki?' I asked.

'It's Monday. I never miss a Monday, child. It's something I've done for years, worshipping at the Paroor temple on a Monday. I don't feel at peace unless I see that deity. I feel that all my sins are washed away when I worship him.'

Devaki stopped grating the coconut and smiled at me.

'Going to the Paroor temple is not enough to wash your sins away!' Sankaran called out to her from the kitchen.

'And what do you mean by that?' asked Devaki. Her smile had suddenly disappeared.

'I don't have to tell you what sins you've committed. I've been seeing you for years, after all. I know what happens and does not happen here. I lie down at night on the wooden chest in the eastern verandah, but I sleep with my eyes open. And my ears as well. I know who goes past the gate, who whistles, everything . . .'

'Don't say things like that. Talking of scandalous matters in front of the child!'

'I didn't say anything scandalous. I wouldn't know how to say scandalous things even if I wanted to! Everyone here knows that. I've been staying in this house and cooking for this family for ages. No one in this village has ever found fault with my conduct. I won't endure it if some woman from Mookkola turns up suddenly and spreads lies about me. I'm going to tell Valiamma.'

'And what are you going to tell her? I have things to tell her too. Women here dare not go out at night to urinate—you're sure to follow . . .'

'I'm a human being too, am I not? What if I need to urinate as well? If you go out, does it mean I can't?'

'There are so many yards here—why do you have to come to the very same yard I go to? I first thought it wasn't deliberate. So I didn't tell Valiamma. But I'm going to tell her now. I can't bear it any more.'

I kept eating grated coconut while Devaki and Sankaran quarrelled. Devaki pushed me aside suddenly.

'Look at her—she's eaten it all! I have to grate some more again. Break a coconut for me.'

Sankaran picked up a coconut from the heap in the corner and shook it vigorously.

'Give her rice to eat and she doesn't want it. Give her milk and she won't drink it. Give her medicine and she'll refuse to have it. But she'll eat all the coconut I can grate! If she has a bad stomach, it's me Valiamma will scold,' muttered Sankaran.

'The parrot that was her friend brought the princess called Chintamani a water melon,' I said.

'I'm fed up of that princess, child. If you've read a story about someone ordinary, tell me that. Can a parrot break open a water melon? Even if it manages to, can it hold the melon and fly? Who prints all these lies? Imagine, the book costs a rupee! If you buy rice for a rupee, you can feed a whole family! Who bought you this book, child? The headmaster? What a waste of money! I don't understand . . .'

'You can't read. Does that mean there's a law that no one else must read? I like that story, child. No matter how many times I hear it, I want to hear Chintamani's story over and over again. Tell me the story, child; I'll never tire

of it. I even like the name: Chintamani. When you grow
up and get married and have a son and then a daughter,
you must call the girl Chintamani. Princess Chintamani.
I'll come and look after the child. We'll do everything to
make sure no one casts an evil eye on the child. We'll
grind herbs for it and tie bells on its waist. We'll dry kunnan
bananas, grind them into powder, mix it in milk and make
a porridge . . .'

'For Chintamani?'

'Yes!'

'How many children will I have?'

Devaki laughed. 'Did you hear the question the child
asked?'

'I heard. I know lots of children here. I know all the
children in my place as well. But never have I come across
a child that talks such nonsense!' said Sankaran.

'Don't ask other people questions like this,' said Devaki.
'It's shameful for an eight-year-old to ask who will marry
me, when will I have babies and all that. There's a time
for everything and everything will happen at the right time.
You can't make it happen before its time.'

'You have to have patience if you're a human being,'
said Sankaran, and Devaki nodded in agreement.
'That's right.'

❖

In olden days, if any woman in the wealthy families in
Punnayoorkulam had an attack of chickenpox or smallpox,
Thoniyare Paru Amma was appointed to look after her.

Pox marks were scattered plentifully over her shining
black skin. Her stout body rolled when she walked, rather
like a ship on an angry sea. Her little brown teeth that
looked like rusty nails were visible only when she smiled,

never while she talked. She always wore well-starched, pristine white clothes.

At least four times a year she would push open the door of the northern verandah and suddenly appear in the vadikkini. I had heard Ammaman's mother say that she had come to Nalapat before I was born, before even my mother was born, to look after someone who fell sick. No one ever told me whether that invalid had survived or died. But in gratitude for that act of kindness, the Nalapat women welcomed her warmly whenever she came, served her tea and snacks and gave her nentran bananas, a new, unbleached mundu and silver rupee coins to take home. Paru Amma's eyes were always reddish and her rough, mannish voice used to frighten me.

One afternoon when she arrived at Nalapat, everyone except me was fast asleep. I was in the thekkini, reading a book with my head against a huge pillar. She pushed open the door to the vadikkini and called out loudly, 'Anyone here?'

Devaki's snores rose from the vadikkini. In the summer month of Medam, everyone would fall asleep after lunch, maybe because of the intensity of the heat. Valiamma and Muthassi were asleep in the thekkini and Cheriamma in the room upstairs. Ammaman slept in the room over the gatehouse and Ammamma in the northern bedroom. Ettan used to spread a mattress on the floor of the central room and sleep there.

Disappointed to see that I was the only one awake, Paru Amma said, 'So you're the only one who's not asleep, child? I need to see Kochu Amma about something. She must be asleep. When will she wake up? I have to go somewhere and I'll get there by dark only if I set off now. That Nethiar Amma's daughter's ill, quite severely ill. I'll have to pluck a whole bunch of neem leaves on the way. When will Kochu Amma wake up? Go and check, child. Tell her that Thoniyare Paru Amma is here. I need two rupees. I can't go to a smallpox patient's house without any money on me: sometimes you can't even find someone there to buy betel leaves. People are scared to look after someone who has smallpox, even if it's their own mother. Often there won't even be anyone around to give them some kanji to drink. It's I who will have to do everything. Everyone in the house would have left and gone off to some relative's place. Usually, there'll be just me and the patient. And they would have left their pots and pans and all their worldly goods behind. Thanks to me, nothing disappears. If it were someone else, they'd lose everything! I would never touch a thing, child. I don't want anything that belongs to others. I'm honest and straight. That's why I'm able to look after people who've caught smallpox. I had it once, when I was just ten. My mother sent all the children away to Cheruthoor and there was no one left to care for me. My mother would come now and then and leave a bowl of kanji on the doorstep for me, that was all. When it grew dark, if I was conscious, I'd go to the compound to relieve myself; otherwise, I'd just do it where I lay . . . I spent four months in bed, child. No one thought I'd live. My face was full of pits and scars and children would be frightened and scream when they caught sight of me! Still, I didn't die. Now I'm of some use to other people. Everyone wants Thoniyare Paru Amma when they fall ill. Once they recover, they don't want me any more. Isn't that human nature? It doesn't make me sad at all . . .'

Paru Amma came right into the thekkini and sat down at the edge of the open courtyard. She wiped her reddish eyes with a corner of her towel.

'My life is dedicated to others, child,' she said, her voice trembling with emotion.

Her tears quietened my fears and I felt the thudding of my heart slow down.

'What do you want, Paru Amma?' I asked.

'Will you give me whatever I want, child?' she asked with a sad smile.

I nodded assent.

'What I want right now is a cup of tea. I've been out in the sun and my head aches badly. Once I have tea, I want to chew some betel leaves with good areca nut and a wad of tobacco. Then I need a small pot of jeera-water. And two rupees to tuck into my waist. Do you think you can give me all this, child?'

She laughed loudly, a laugh that reminded me of crows crackling their wings noisily as they fought for morsels of food by the well. A mingled gasp and laugh.

'I'll call Ammamma,' I said.

'Won't your Ammamma scold you if you wake her up suddenly?' asked Paru Amma.

'No, Ammamma won't scold me,' I said.

I woke up Ammamma and told her Paru Amma had come to see her. She was not at all pleased.

'Did she touch you, Kamala?' she asked in a low voice.
'No.'

'You sit here then, Kamala. I'll give her the money.'

'I want to see Paru Amma,' I said.

'No! She's been looking after smallpox patients. It's a contagious disease.' Ammamma hurried down the stairs. I lay down flat on the mat spread on the verandah, listening to what Ammamma and Paru Amma said to each other downstairs. I couldn't make out all the words. I was unhappy that I could not see Paru Amma from there.

'I heard she's nineteen. It's hard to recover if one gets it at that age. You have to be a small child or a withered, shrivelled old woman—then you will survive. You have to observe strict quarantine if you go down with this disease.'

❖

It was past midnight when Paatti Cheeru and her group arrived at Nalapat to play the thukil and wake all of us out of our sleep. I woke up as soon as I heard the sound of the thukil, clear and cold as rainwater. Panan men who had tufts of hair on their heads took over the refrain of her song.

I sold the land, children,
To eat the Onam feast
I'll play the thukil now
And wake you up,
Oh great Thrikkakkara God . . .

I hurried down the stairs and went to the southern verandah. The yard lay bathed in moonlight. It was a season when all the trees were in bloom: the kanhira in the snake shrine, the pari, the ilanji, the kumkumam and even the Rangoon creeper that had wound itself around the neermathalam tree. The south-western breeze wafted in the fragrance of the flowers.

Paatti Cheeru was a short, dark woman. Her sleek, well-oiled hair was gathered into a tight chignon and her full breasts were covered with a newly washed towel. As soon as she caught sight of me, Paatti Cheeru stopped singing for a minute to smile brightly at me. I had heard my mother and grandmother often speak of the seductive nature of her voice. Bala, the daughter of the washerwoman Lakshmikutty, had a high regard for Paatti Cheeru.

While I leaned back against Ammamma, who was seated on a grass mat in the verandah, and listened to Paatti

Cheeru singing, I saw a star fall down from the southern sky. It was the first time ever that I saw a star fall.

'A star has fallen into our yard,' I said.

'I saw it too. It fell into the pond,' said Sankaran.

'Into our pond?' asked Devaki.

'Shh . . .' Muthassi looked displeased as she hushed them.

'Can you take it out?' I asked Sankaran.

'Not now, child. I can't see at night. I'll look for it in the morning. It may burn my hand, but that doesn't matter. If we take it out and keep it in your room, child, you won't need a lamp at night.'

'Shh . . .' said Ammamma, 'I can't hear her sing with all of you talking. Can't you be quiet?'

I woke up the next morning thinking about the star that had fallen into the pond. I went to the southern verandah to clean my mouth and found that Sankaran had had a bath and was already in the kitchen, a line of sandal paste gleaming on his forehead.

'Did you get it, Sankara?' I asked.

'Get what?'

'The star that fell from the sky last night.'

'No, I didn't find it. I looked for it a long time under the water. All I found was the lid of Valiamma's soapbox, a bright red one. Look at it.'

Sankaran held out the lid with a smile. I could not bear to think that he had found the lid of a soapbox instead of a star!

'Che, couldn't you have left it there?' I asked.

'Leave it there? What are you saying, child? Valiamma can cover her soapbox now, can't she? Smell it, child. It smells of tortoises and water snakes.'

'Throw it away,' said Devaki. 'If the child touches it, her hands will smell too.'

'Will the star smell of water snakes?'

'A bit. If a star lies in the water, tortoises and water snakes are sure to go and lick it—to find out whether they can eat it, you know,' said Sankaran.

'How big will it be?' I asked.

'Didn't you see it when it fell? It's as big as the deep plate you have your broken-rice kanji in. It's so beautiful that you'd think it's a silver plate! I couldn't find it today since I didn't have time. When I woke up, child, it was morning already. I have to light the fire before Valiamma wakes up and comes down, don't I? The star won't get lost. It could have fallen on the edge of the pond, where the yellow arali grows wild. The baby waterfowl live there. The star could have fallen on them. What a nuisance this star is! If it fell on the baby waterfowl, they would have died!' said Sankaran.

'You keep telling the child lies to make her cry. Don't you have anything else to do?' Devaki raised her voice. She broke off a broomstick from the young coconut palm growing by the side of the well and split it down the centre.

'Scrape your tongue with this, child. Don't listen to his lies. It's getting late. Stars don't fall into ponds,' said Devaki.

'I saw it fall,' I said.

'That wasn't a star. It must have been a cracker someone lighted—haven't you seen the fireworks people light for Vishu? It couldn't have been a star,' said Devaki.

'Oh yes, a cracker indeed! Whoever heard of fireworks in the month of Chingam? Go and ask Valiamma—she saw the star fall. It whizzed over the snake shrine with a hissing sound. You know the sound a drop of water makes when it falls into a hot frying pan? That's the sound we heard. When we peered out, we saw a star fall into the pond.'

'All right, all right, maybe the star is still lying in the pond. Go and get it. The child believes all the lies you tell and then she asks Valiamma and the master about them. She'll ask them now whether they saw the star fall into the pond. And it's I who will be scolded. They'll think it's I who told her these stories. And they'll scold me till there's nothing left of me! Don't you know, Amina Umma once told the child about some way to prevent people casting the evil eye on her. And the child went straight to the front portico to tell the master! The master sprang up and asked, "Who taught you this, Aami"? The child began to shiver with fear and Valiamma was frightened as well. The child wouldn't mention Amina Umma's name. The master glared at me so angrily that I pissed in fright! I thought he'd thrash me. So I ran away and hid in the shed near the pond. The master will want to know now who taught the child all these silly things. And it's me he'll drive out of the place, not you!' said Devaki. She sprinkled water on my face and wiped it dry with a towel.

'I'm not in the habit of telling lies. I saw that star fall with my own eyes. Ask the people at Mambulli house—one of them may have seen it fall. The star whizzed through their yard, after all. Ask Valli, she'll tell you that I never talk about things I haven't seen with my own eyes. The child saw it too. I remember, it was when Paatti Cheeru was singing the story of Darikan that the star fell into the pond,' said Sankaran.

'Will you look for it again?' I asked Sankaran.

'There are people who drain ponds. You just have to give them two rupees. They'll scoop out all the dirt and scum in the pond. They did that the other day in the pond at Marathattu and found a bell-metal ladle. Mannanthara Gopalan Nair told me about it—so don't say now that it's one of my lies!' said Sankaran.

'So you'll have to drain the pond then, to find the star? Are you crazy or something? The child will go and tell the master straightaway that the pond has to be drained to find

the star. And the master will drive me out. Because it's I
who look after her—she's my responsibility, isn't she? Your
responsibility is the kitchen. Light the firewood and cook
the dal—that's what you're paid to do. And I'll take care of
the child. Do you understand that?' asked Devaki angrily.

'Why must you shout? Valiamma will come rushing here
now to find out what's wrong. I sometimes think you're
not human!' said Sankaran.

'What am I then if I'm not human?'

'You're a demoness, like Tataka!'

Devaki's eyes suddenly filled with tears. She bent down
and wiped her eyes with a corner of her mundu.

'I have to behave like a demon now and then because
the child is in my charge. That's not my fault,' she said.

'I'm not saying it's your fault. I'm just telling you what I
saw. Last night, I saw the star fall. The child saw it too. I
thought it fell into the pond. What's wrong with that? I'm
not doing anyone any harm. Is it wrong to talk about
something one has seen? Tell me if it is—then I won't talk
of it any more. I'm not educated or rich. If I were, would I
be working as a cook? I'm tired of pushing sticks of firewood
into the hearth endlessly. Sometimes I think I should go
and sow paddy in the fields, or join the army. I'm tired of
making rice and sambhar, tired of lighting the fire, on and
on. I no longer know who I am . . .' said Sankaran.

I saw that Sankaran's eyes too had filled with tears.

'Why are you crying, Sankara?' I asked.

'I'm not crying, child. When I opened the container of
chilli powder to measure out some for the chutney, I think
a speck of the powder went into my eye,' said Sankaran.

'Is it burning? Shall I blow into your eye? I asked.

'No, little one. Don't do that. Sankaran is happy you
thought of doing that for him, that's all he wants. Once
you go back to Calcutta, child, I won't stay here even for a

day. There's no one I feel more loyal to than to you. I don't say that people here are not good. And it's true that none of the horrible things that happen in other houses ever take place here. And I'm happy here. But how can one spend a whole life lighting the fire? I'm doing a woman's work here. Scraping coconut, draining rice, making dosas: they're all women's tasks. Sowing in the fields is a man's job, as is turning the soil at the foot of a coconut palm. I want to spend the rest of my days doing a man's job,' said Sankaran.

'Go and do Anjakalan's work then. We'll see how thin and weak you'll become. I've seen you keeping aside some thick kanji when you drain the rice. And I've watched you add coconut milk to it, go off to a dark corner and gulp it down. If you start digging around the coconut palms, your pot belly will disappear in no time and you'll grow thin and weak. Your skin will turn dark. Don't say I didn't warn you. Think well before you go and work in the fields!' said Devaki, laughing.

'All right then, I'll work in the kitchen a little longer. I don't want you to feel that I didn't listen to you. But I'm certain of one thing: I saw that star fall into the pond with my own eyes. You can't say that's a lie. I feel my heart breaking with sorrow when you say that. I've had to tell lies sometimes. But this isn't one. This is something I really saw. It sprang from the top of the kanhira tree in the snake shrine, came flying through the yard of the Mambulli family and fell into our pond! And it made a hissing sound as it fell. I heard it. Don't say it's a lie. My heart will break,' said Sankaran, his voice quivering.

Devaki said nothing. She suddenly gave me a loving hug.

❖

I did not know until Valli told me that Unnimayamma used to meet an extremely handsome gandharva on moonlit evenings in the vicinity of her house, under the palmyra on the edge of the pond.

'They say the gandharva is as tall as coconut palm!' said Valli.

'I want to see him too—take me to Mannanthara,' I said. Valli spat out saliva stained red with betel juice and laughed.

'That's just an old story. There are no gandharvas or yakshis now. Do you know what you'll see under the coconut palm now?' asked Valli.

'What will I see?'

'Dog shit! The shit of the dogs that the Mannanthara people rear. Don't go there to see that! I was just talking of an old story . . .'

Around that period, two dogs belonging to the Mannanthara family used to come in through the broken fence at Nalapat and stand in the northern yard, wagging their tails. Mud-coloured creatures, begging for food. Sankaran sometimes gave them dosas or sweet appams and sometimes threw stones at them.

'If you want to see a yakshi, stand under the palm on the northern side of the house. She comes there on moonlit nights. With her hair flying loose, an enchanting seductress. Dark red lips, a round pottu of chandu on her forehead and an ilakkuri. Each of her breasts is as huge as a jackfruit. Once you see her, you'll never forget her!' said Valli.

'Have you seen a yakshi, Valli?' I asked.

'No, I haven't. Where do I have the time to stand and look at yakshis? I have to give my children their kanji. Their father has a rumble in his chest all the time. You can hear the sound of him wheezing, kru, kru . . . He grows very restless around full moon and I have to heat rice-bran poultices for him. I don't have any spare time at all. I'm telling you frankly, it's men that yakshis like. They never let go of handsome men. Haven't you heard the story of how a yakshi killed a Namboodiri and drank his blood? It took place near our place, in Edappal. You must have read about it in the papers in Calcutta. You couldn't have missed it.'

'I didn't read about it.'

'Listen then. Two Namboodiris were on their way to the Guruvayoor temple. One of them was very handsome. When they came to Edappal, they saw this enchantress coming over the fields. Her hair lying loose, her lips reddened, her large breasts dancing as she moved. The yakshi asked the Namboodiri, "Will you give me some lime paste?" Then . . .'

'Don't frighten the child, Valli. What stories you tell!' Sankaran said crossly.

'I want to hear Valli's story,' I said.

'The child will scream in her sleep if she listens to this story. And it's Sankaran who'll be scolded. You go away in the evening, Valli, and it's I who'll be shouted at. Don't you realize that?' said Sankaran.

'First of all,' said Devaki, 'there's no such thing as a yakshi. Secondly, this event took place in my village, in Nannammukku. I've seen the Namboodiri. He's such a good-looking man!'

'How on earth could you have seen a dead Namboodiri? The yakshi killed him and drank his blood. Did he get up then and come down from heaven to Nannammukku to see you?' asked Valli.

'The Namboodiri in my story doesn't have to be the one in yours,' said Devaki.

'Don't you have anything except yakshi stories to tell the child?' asked Sankaran.

'Haven't you seen yakshis, Sankaran Kammal?' asked Valli.

'No, I haven't. How wonderful if I could see one! She would keep me company. When I feel cold at night during the Thiruvathira season, I can hold her tight in my arms.'

'Ai, ai, what things you say in front of the child! Have you no shame?' asked Devaki.

'I was just wishing aloud. Let the child hear. I wanted to be frank. I hope a yakshi comes to marry me. Shouldn't I get married too? There's no law, is there, that I can't get married just because I don't have any money?'

'When will you marry the yakshi, Sankara?' I asked eagerly.

'During the next Onam festival. Our wedding will take place in the sky. There's a yakshi waiting for me in the sky, with a full measure of paddy and a lighted brass lamp before her.'

'It's a lie, child. Don't believe him,' said Devaki.

I looked up at the sky. Between the huge branches of the mango tree, I saw fragments of sky that resembled the broken shards of a blue glass bowl.

'The yakshi wears a freshly washed mundu that's been dipped in blue. A white mundu with a narrow border. She doesn't wear a blouse. She wears beautiful necklaces in traditional designs. Your two mortal eyes are not enough to see all of her, child!' said Sankaran.

'Will you call her "yakshi", Sankara?'

'No, child. Once I marry her, she won't answer if I call her "yakshi". So I'll call her Ammu. My Ammukutty.' Overcome with emotion, Sankaran flung his arms around the pillar on the verandah.

'You're mad,' said Valli, laughing.

'Ammu, Ammukutty,' whispered Sankaran to the pillar.

'It all comes of not getting married at the right time. Did you see how he's hugging the pillar and whispering "Ammu" to it, like a madman? Can't you tell Valiamma frankly that you want to get married? Devaki Amral is the same caste as you. The right age too,' said Valli.

'Valli, I don't need you to fix up a marriage for me,' said Devaki.

'When will you get married if not now? After you're past the childbearing age?'

'Don't worry about my having children, Valli.'

'People are talking about you. So many people ask me whether you and Sankaran Kammal are having a secret love affair.'

'A secret love affair? Who asked you? Tell me, whoever it is. I'll give them an answer. I'm sure there are women in this village who have secret love affairs. But women from my place have never indulged in such nonsense, nor will they ever do so. If you spread rumours like that, my uncle will not spare you. He's a really hot-tempered man. Women should either sit quiet in their houses, or attend to their jobs if they go out to work. My uncle will kill anyone who spreads stories about me. There's no one who hasn't heard of him in our parts. He's a fierce, vengeful man . . . do you understand?'

'What are you going on and on about? What's so shameful about people talking of you and me in that way? I'm a Nair, after all. My only drawback is that I was born in a poor family. But I'm not one of those inferior Velakathara or Pallichan Nairs—I'm a real Kiriyath Nair! If it's a rich husband you're hoping for, tell me so and I'll withdraw. Not only I but the whole village knows that there are some Menons running after you—men wearing silk shirts and watches and reeking of perfume. It's been going on for quite some time. And one of these days, the

Menons will all go away pretending nothing has happened. It's you who'll have to face the music. I'm telling you because I feel sorry for you. I can't think of any other way to rescue you except to marry you!' said Sankaran.

'Say yes, Devaki Amral,' urged Valli. 'It's difficult to survive here without a man as companion. Come evening, there are demon-like types that come out to catch hold of women. Cruel creatures. They use young girls and throw them away like one chews sugar cane and spits out the dry fibre. Sometimes you see corpses surfacing in the well or bodies beaten to death hanging on mango trees. Who's to ask what happened when the victims are all poor people . . . Marry Sankaran Kammal quickly and then you'll have a husband to protect you.'

Sankaran was stretched out on the wooden chest, pretending to be asleep. I saw the pupils move under his closed eyelids.

'You're awake, aren't you, Sankara?' I asked. Tears spilled out from beneath his eyelids.

'Sankaran is crying,' I announced.

'It's just pretence,' said Valli. 'Don't worry.'

'Who has been spreading falsehoods about me?' Devaki asked Valli.

'No one. They're telling the truth. There's someone who follows you around all the time: a man in a silk shirt, who wears a watch and reeks of perfume, just like Sankaran Kammal said. A gandharva. He doesn't want that gandharva to betray you, that's all. He doesn't want you to be ruined, doesn't want your corpse to surface in a well,' said Valli. Devaki sank to the ground, leaned her head on her hands and wept.

'I'm a helpless woman. Anyone would find it easy to deceive me. He's behind me all the time. Yesterday, when I went to pluck flowers, he gave me a letter. I don't know how to read. But I was afraid to throw away the letter in the yard. So I tucked it into my waist. When I finished mopping the floor and looked for it, I couldn't find it. I don't know into whose hands it fell. If they kick me out of this place, where will I go? I'm not a bad woman, Valli. People follow me around and then say I'm bad. I've only the goddess, Mookkola Bhagavathi, to protect me. You know I don't have parents. If I'm thrown into a well, there'll be no one to ask where I am!'

'Won't your uncle come and ask for you?'

'He's dead, isn't he? But no one will bother about me if they know he's dead. That's why I make up all kinds of stories about him. Actually, no one will care even if I'm murdered!'

Devaki's sobbing troubled me.

'You have me, don't you, Devaki?' I said, putting my arms around her.

'That's true. Go with her to Calcutta, Amral. The rogues in this village won't ever come there.'

'Take me too with you, child,' said Sankaran, sitting up.

'Why, are you afraid as well?'

'I think they're going to beat me up here. I believe *he*, that other fellow, said he'd get the Vettuvans to thrash me. Do you know who told me? That mad Parvathi's mother.'

'But she can't speak. Then how did she tell you all this?'

'I understand everything that those madwomen say. It's not just mad people who talk to me—crows, cats, cattle, dogs, they all talk to me. And I understand what they say.'

'Teach me the crow-language,' I said.

'All right, I will. This Sankaran will teach you. In return, you must teach me English.'

Devaki wiped her eyes and laughed. So did I.

❖

One evening, Sankaran did not come back from the market even after dusk. Since the pappadams he always brought back had not arrived, dinner was not ready for us children. As soon as the first star was visible at dusk, Ammamma used to serve Ettan and me our meal: fine broken rice, seasoned buttermilk, bitter-gourd wafers, salted mangoes and pappadams roasted over hot coals. We waited sadly in the eastern verandah, staring outside, wondering why Sankaran was not back as yet.

'What could have happened? Sankaran never comes back so late,' said Ammamma, holding up the hurricane lantern to peer out. Shadows moved to and fro behind the Nalapat gatehouse, among the lime trees in the yard and on the edge of the fields. They were not the shadows of human beings but of the swaying branches of trees.

'I think someone is coming from the side of the carpenters' workshed. Kamala, go and look—see if it's Sankaran,' said Ammamma.

'Why are you so worried, Valiamma, that he hasn't returned? He's not a little child, after all. He turned twenty-six last year. Listening to Valiamma, you'd think he's an infant who'll trip and fall on the roadside!' said Devaki loudly, her voice shrill with displeasure.

'Why are you so worried, Kochu? He must be at Poozhikkalam, watching a trapeze act or something,' said Muthassi.

'It's nearly eight! Trapeze act indeed! Who would come to watch if they had one at this time of the night?' asked Ammamma.

'You don't know, Valiamma. They have bright lamps like the one we use in the front room in all the shops in Poozhikkalam. Petromaxes. When you walk past them, you feel it's day, not night!' said Devaki.

'When did you go to Poozhikkalam, Devaki?' asked Ammamma.

'I didn't go, Valiamma. Valli told me about them. I never go anywhere. Nor do I wish to. How many times . Valli has said, "Come with me to Poozhikkalam, Amral." I don't want to. Never in my life will I go to places where rogues hang around. I went once, for Guruvayoor Ekadashi. And had enough! Never again will Devaki go gallivanting . . .'

'Did Sankaran tell you he would be late?' asked Muthassi.

'How strange! Why should it matter to me if he comes late? I'm not his wife, am I? Why should he tell me he'll be late coming back?' Devaki gesticulated wildly as she spoke.

'How can I serve Ettan's meal without pappadams . . .?' lamented Ammamma.

Sankaran came in through the gate at that moment. Blood dripped down the right side of his face, his hands and shoulders. He collapsed on the ground.

'Whatever happened, Sankara?' asked Ammamma frenziedly.

'I couldn't make out anything in the dark, Valiamma.'

'Who threw stones at you, Sankara?' asked Muthassi.

'I can't tell you their names. They're bigwigs after all, and used to beating people to death and throwing their bodies in the well! I won't say a word, or give any names. Early morning tomorrow, I'm leaving this place. I'll go to my own village and work there for a daily wage. No one will have me thrashed by goondas there. I don't want to get married, or earn a salary, or anything! I'll eke out a living at home with my people,' said Sankaran.

Devaki's face grew pale. But she did not say a word. She just stood there, leaning against the wall. Ammamma turned to her angrily.

'Don't stand there like that. Go and get some sugar,' she said to Devaki.

'Shouldn't we send for the apothecary, Kochu?' asked Muthassi.

Ammamma ran her fingers through Sankaran's hair.

'It's not a very deep cut. Let me put sugar on it. We have to stop the bleeding,' said Ammamma.

Ammamma pressed sugar firmly into the wounds. Sankaran said, 'Some water . . .'

Devaki brought him cold water in a vessel with a spout. Sankaran refused to touch it.

Ammamma brought him water mixed with sugar in a bell-metal glass. Sankaran gulped it down quickly.

'Do you want some milk, Sankara?' asked Ammamma.

'Have your dinner and go to bed, Sankara,' said Muthassi.

'I have a terrible headache. I don't feel like eating at all,' muttered Sankaran.

'Don't sleep on the floor. If it gets cold at night, you'll have rheumatism,' said Ammamma.

Ammamma helped Sankaran lie down on the wooden chest on which he generally slept at night.

'I feel a little better now, Valiamma. I'll get up in the morning and milk the cow,' said Sankaran. A feeble smile appeared on his face.

'Is it hurting, Sankara?' I asked.

'No, little one. It's stopped hurting now. Don't be sad, little one.'

'Who made people throw stones at you, Sankara?' I asked. Sankaran looked at Devaki.

'I don't know, little one,' he said.

'Do you have an enemy, Sankara?' asked Muthassi.

'I've not harmed anyone,' said Sankaran.

'Don't talk too much now. It will tire you. You can tell us everything tomorrow,' said Ammamma.

I woke up in the middle of the night hearing Ammamma's voice. She had got up from the bed we shared and gone to the verandah. She said to Muthassi, 'We'll have to send her away. If we let her stay on here, I've no idea what the consequences will be, Amma.'

'I've never found anything wrong with her behaviour. If we listen to what people say and dismiss the poor thing, won't her curses haunt us? Think well, Kochu, before you do that. Do whatever you think is right,' said Muthassi.

'What I wish to do is protect Sankaran,' said Ammamma.

I got up and went to the verandah. Ammamma hastily scrambled up from the floor. Her hair was tied in a knot over her head.

'Is Sankaran all right now?' I asked.

'I didn't check. Let me go and have a look,' said Ammamma.

'Stay here, Kamala. Don't go to the front verandah,' said Muthassi.

'Is it nearly morning?' I asked.

'No, it must be just past midnight.'

Ammamma went down the stairs. I could hear her footsteps going through the thekkini first, then the vadikkini. Then I heard her ask Devaki, 'Why are you sitting here? Aren't you sleepy, Devaki?'

Devaki sobbed, 'Never in all my life will I be able to sleep again!'

'Why is Devaki crying?' I asked Muthassi.

'She must be thinking about Sankaran,' said Muthassi.

'Won't Sankaran's wounds heal?' I asked.

'Of course they will.'

'Sankara . . .' called Ammamma loudly from the southern yard. Muthassi, I and everyone else went rushing down the stairs. There was no one on the wooden chest.

'Why are you looking so worried, Kochu?' asked Muthassi.

I saw a crescent moon gleaming above the date palm that stood at the edge of the well.

'Just look at where Sankaran was sleeping, Amma— there's only a pool of blood there,' said Ammamma. 'I wonder whether someone has carried him off.'

'He must have gone to relieve himself. Don't panic, Kochu. I'm sure he'll go to the pond, wash himself and come back. He'll be all right. Don't get worked up over nothing,' said Muthassi.

'I'm sure that's what it is,' said Cheriamma.

'He might have gone home to his family,' said Devaki. 'He's been saying he wants to go for quite a few days. He's been restless ever since he recovered the money from the chit fund last month. Running to and fro aimlessly. . . He's bought a bolt of unbleached cloth and he told me he wanted to buy a lot more material for clothes. Yesterday afternoon he was talking about having a green chintz shirt tailored.'

'He'd never go without telling me,' said Ammamma.

'Wait till it's morning, Kochu. We'll send Anjakalan to Sankaran's village. Devaki is right. He said he wanted to get married—he was in a great hurry. Maybe he went home, like Devaki said.'

Ammamma flashed the torch into the yard. 'Aren't those drops of blood?' she asked.

'I don't see anything,' muttered Muthassi.

'They're pavizhamalli flowers,' said Cheriamma.

❖

Ammaman's mother's name was Madhavikutty Amma. But from the time I could remember, everyone used to call her

Nalapat Valia Valiamma. She did not have the pale skin
that all the Nalapat women had. The senior bhattadirippad
of Kattumadom, a reputed practitioner of black magic, was
her father. She must have inherited her brown-toned skin,
her deep-set eyes and the haughty expression on her face
from him. She did not like to speak much. She would repeat
'Namah Shivaya, Namah Shivaya' to herself endlessly. She
wore a long chain of tulasi beads set in gold.

When she developed a severe stomach ache that would
not subside, the little cupboard that held sugar and tea in
the room on the east was moved outside. Valiamma's cot
was moved to the centre of the room, next to the pillar
and the eastern room thus became a room for invalids to
rest in. Valiamma lay on her back, staring with half-closed
eyes through the eastern window at the blue beetles
humming as they circled around the bean creeper.
Dr Bhaskaran gave her an injection of morphine to relieve
her pain. The doctor told her relatives that she had cancer
and would never recover.

When Valiamma died, her body was wrapped in a
length of unbleached jagannathan cloth. Four people
carried her to the southern yard. A huge branch of the
mango tree from which the swing hung was lopped off to
prepare the pyre to burn her body. Watching Valiamma
go on her last journey, her son, my grand-uncle, who was
confined to bed, a victim of diabetic sores, lost control of
himself and wept like a small child.

'Amma, my mother!' I felt distressed to see him weep
so bitterly, the person who used to comfort us children
when we wept. I realized there was no point ever expecting
Ammaman to protect us again. I could not bear the thought
that even this man, who was known as a scholar and
philosopher, had to bow his head before death.

'Ammaman cannot bring dead people back to life, can he?' I asked Ammamma.

'Don't say silly things, Kamala,' muttered Ammamma.

'Jesus Christ made Lazarus live again. Can't Ammaman similarly bring Valiamma back to life?'

'Jesus Christ lived in another era. This is Kaliyuga and no one can bring the dead back to life,' said Ammamma in a stern voice, refusing to continue the discussion.

We had a new cook called Ravunni Nair. He had no interest in spiritual matters. He used to finish cooking well before dusk and go back home. Ammamma used to warm the food and serve it to us.

One day, I said grumpily, 'I prefer the sambhar Sankaran used to make.'

'Sankaran used to indulge the child's every wish. That's why she says his sambhar was good. It's not because your sambhar is not good, Ravunni Nair,' said Ammamma.

Ravunni Nair grunted, glaring balefully at me.

'Sankaran used to tell jokes and do funny things to make the children laugh,' said Muthassi.

Ravunni Nair placed an areca nut that had been skinned on the grinding stone and chopped it into tiny morsels. Every time he raised the knife to bring it down, he grunted heavily and his tuft quivered.

Changes came about in the room on the northern side, where Devaki slept as well. Newcomers, a middle-aged woman named Madhavi Amma and a young girl named Meenakshikutty, arranged their bags and boxes neatly in two corners. Madhavi Amma was a splendid beauty with cheeks the colour of sunrise. Her earrings were shaped like the wheels of the Sun God's chariot. With kajal in her eyes, yellow sandal paste and a red pottu above it on her forehead and her hair gathered high behind her head like a snake's hood, she wandered in and out of the house and through the compound, supervising the servants. Soon, people going to the market through the fields, or to bathe in the river in Eliyangode by the path under the punna tree began to linger awhile to turn and look at her. And once they looked at her, they turned again and again to stare. From which palace, they wondered, had this newly arrived princess come? This peacock that pirouetted in the western yard of Nalapat in the mellow evening sunlight in her bright green blouse and her starched white mundu with a narrow border, as if to show off her graceful gait . . .

Madhavi Amma made the servants do all the household chores. No one ever dared ask her to do any herself. Servants who never bothered to listen to any instructions the Nalapat women gave them obeyed Madhavi Amma implicitly. She kept her distance from everyone. Only a woman named Velakathara Kalyani somehow became the object of Madhavi Amma's affection. They often spent time together in the tiled shed over the bathing tank at Nalapat. Kalyani had obviously undertaken the tasks of massaging Madhavi Amma's body with oil and rubbing perfumed oil into her hair. The shed was usually locked from inside. But I could make out that slightly mannish voice even when I stood under the ilanji tree directly outside. Madhavi Amma would describe to Kalyani the greatness of the people of the Kaprasserry taravad or the strange habits that Brahmins had. Kalyani did not always agree with everything she said. But her parrot-voice would intone at the end of every sentence Madhavi Amma spoke, 'Oh my God, what is this I hear!'

Meenakshi had a companion in Unnimaya's younger sister, Padmavathi, and also in Parukutty, the newest bride in the Mambulli family. For the first time, young girls joked and laughed in Nalapat.

'Finish your work, girls, instead of giggling all the time,' Ravunni Nair would scold. 'These creatures don't need an excuse to start giggling. If I tell them to husk a coconut, they grin; if I tell them to smear cow dung on the floor, they grin; I tell them to mix the cattle feed and give it to the cows and it sets them giggling again!' Ravunni Nair's voice was full of contempt.

'Let them laugh if they want to,' said Valli, trying to pacify Ravunni Nair. 'This is their time to laugh, isn't it? Will they laugh when they grow old? They don't have any cares now. They can eat their fill. Let them laugh—how long will they be able to?'

'What about the person who was sent away from here? Her time for laughter and playfulness is over, isn't it? Nobody here talks about her any more. That's why I said this grinning will bring them no good. If they are quiet and submissive, someone will marry them and take them away. If that doesn't happen, they'll earn a bad name. It's old women who should advise the young. Can't you advise them, Valli? One of them got herself a bad name. And a good man died because of a woman, didn't he?' Ravunni Nair moved his index finger agitatedly.

'Don't say he died! If he did, shouldn't there have been a corpse? He must have gone off somewhere,' said Valli.

'Indeed! He must have gone to Kashi to wash away his sins! I don't want to listen to this nonsense. It's not the first time someone has gone missing like this in this area. And there'll be more and more who are missing. If people lose their heads and try playing tricks on the wealthy, their families won't even see their dead bodies! That's why I say it's better that young girls lead quiet and modest lives, or the next thing you know, their corpses will surface in a well!' roared Ravunni Nair.

Glass bangles tinkled in the grinding shed, in the washing area around the well, in the cowshed . . .

Seated on the bamboo swing hung from the mango tree, I thought of Valiamma's eyes every time I rose towards the blue sky. I felt that another strong push with my foot would take me to the cloud-gate of the world Valiamma now lived in.

When I went to Marathattu one afternoon to play, Kaveri Oppu, a relative of Thangam's father, was seated on the western verandah talking to the stone worker, Mathiri.

'Do the people of your caste believe that there's another world?' asked Kaveri Oppu.

'Another world? What's that? Aren't you with God once you die? God will not abandon believers.'

'God brought the dead Lazarus back to life!' I said.

A smile lighted up Mathiri's face. 'How did you know that, child?' she asked, astonished.

'She must have learned it at the convent in Thrissur,' said Kaveri Oppu. 'What's the point of teaching Hindus these things? Malathikutty came away from there. She didn't like the food or the prayers or the rules. She cried and cried and came away.'

'But *you* managed there without crying, didn't you, child?' asked Mathiri.

'Kamala is very brave. Malathikutty's not like that. She can't live without Kutti Oppu,' said Kaveri Oppu.

'Thangam of Kottayam has come of age,' said Mathiri. 'She's just eleven!'

'She has a well-developed body. I saw her last week at Govindapuram and thought to myself, she looks big enough to come of age. Kamala and Thangam here keep getting smaller and smaller! They look like baby rats. They don't eat properly—then how will they put on flesh?'

I bowed my head, conscious of being inferior to Thangam of Kottayam.

'Look at this Ambazhathel girl here and learn from her. Do you think girls are worth looking at unless they have a bit of flesh on their bones?' Mathiri's question was addressed to both Thangam and me.

Thangam's mother opened the window. 'Maybe she's thin, but our Thangam here will be the first to come of age, that's for sure.'

'How can you be so sure?'

'Wait and see. Our Thangam will be the first . . .'

'Come of age . . . what does that mean?' I asked.

They all laughed. Thangam's mother hushed them and pointed her index finger in warning. 'Father's asleep upstairs.'

'I don't think anything has been explained to this child. She'll be afraid now and start to weep when something happens,' said Mathiri.

'Do girls have to be taught about coming of age?' asked Kaveri Oppu.

'That's what they should be taught. What's the use of teaching them arithmetic? Every evening I see Francis and Kochanna light a kerosene lamp and sit down on the verandah. One twos are two, two twos are four, they go. They're taught geography, history and English. The only thing they're not taught is ways of making a little money. It seems undignified to teach that. Why don't children like doing the same job their father does?' asked Mathiri.

'Let them study. If Kochakku and Roru want to educate their children, let them. Why does that distress you, Mathiri?' asked Kaveri Oppu.

'Mathiri is right,' said Malathikutty.

'Tell them that, child. The price of these geography and history books would buy us a measure of paddy,' said Mathiri.

'If you get married, Mathiri, and have a child, won't you send it to school? Or will you only teach it how to plaster and whitewash walls?' asked Thangam.

'But I'm not yet married,' said Mathiri, suddenly looking shy.

'Is Kochakku looking out for a boy for you?' asked Kaveri Oppu.

'Can you find one so easily? You have to give gold, cooking vessels and a whole lot of money besides to get a bridegroom!' said Mathiri.

'It's because parents can't afford all this that their girls run away with boys,' said Kaveri Oppu.

'Remember that Maria—she ran away to Bangalore with Raman's son. And the whole family earned a bad name!'

'Why do you say that? Maria and Krishnan fell in love. What's wrong with that?'

'How can you ask me that? Maria's family is such an old one, don't you know? And she ran away with a Thiya boy! Who should be ashamed? Think and tell me. We were all ashamed. No one will ever come forward now to marry a girl from a Nasrani family in Punnayoorkulam,' said Mathiri.

'So what you're saying, Mathiri, is that you'll never get married, yes?' teased Kaveri Oppu, laughing.

'I'm not all that keen on getting married. I get enough to live on by working on the site. I can look after myself— I don't need anyone's help,' said Mathiri agitatedly.

'Shh . . .' said Thangam, 'if Father wakes up, we'll all be scolded.'

❖

It was the month of Karkatakam and Ittiyachan's goat was missing. Many people said that some wicked man must have killed it to make soup with its head so that he could drink it and improve his health. Those were the days, besides, when Punnayoorkulam was full of people who suffered from headaches and rheumatic pains. Karkatakam was the month when the potency of all medicines was at its highest. The month when women of wealthy families rubbed mukkuttu oil over their bodies, smeared a layer of raw turmeric over the oil, waited half an hour and then had a bath in warm water. The month when those who were used to eating meat made soup with gizzard and liver every evening, sprinkled pepper and fried onions over it and gulped it down. Everyone knows that the secret of the beauty that reveals itself in women in the month of Chingam lies in the oil baths and medicines they take in Karkatakam, the previous month. It was probably because she knew all this that Ittiyachan's wife, Maria, ran all over the neighbourhood on her long, spindly legs, looking for her goat. She cried out for it constantly and asked so many people whether they had seen it that her voice grew hoarse.

'Lakshmikutty Amma, did my goat go this way?'

Veluthedathu Lakshmikutty Amma was seated on the edge of the pond, cleaning her teeth with tooth powder. Bala and I were gathering the parichaka flowers blooming near the fence. All three of us turned to stare at Maria. I knew at once that she had set out to look for the goat as soon as she woke up, without even washing her face. The usually gracious expression on her face was not there and, doubtless because she was so anxious, her lips looked pale.

'My goat is lost. It had been tied in the shed, but it was not there in the morning. Neither the goat nor the rope was there.'

'I haven't seen your goat for days. Last month I plucked a lot of leaves from the jackfruit tree for it to eat. It was wandering around our compound that day with its rope trailing behind,' said Lakshmikutty.

'Did you see my goat, Bala? Mary's father said he wouldn't let me back in the house if I don't find it.'

'I didn't see it anywhere,' said Bala. Maria went next to the Mambulli house. I followed her.

'Valli, my goat is lost! I tied it up at night in the shed. Neither the goat nor its rope was there in the morning.'

'You know it's Karkatakam. Someone must have stolen it to make soup with its legs,' said Valli. Valli's sons, Raghavan and Prabhakaran, laughed loudly.

'Your goat would have turned into soup by now!' said Prabhakaran.

'Don't say such wicked things! It's thanks to that goat that Mary's father and the children are able to eat some rice and fish curry every night. We supply milk to the tea shop at the corner of the street. Three quarters of a measure. I buy a handul of sardine with the money I get for it. If I don't go back with the goat, he'll throw me out of the house!'

'Who will?' asked Valli.

'How can you ask that? Don't you know what Mary's father is like?'

'Don't tell lies. Ittiyachan is such a meek soul. He doesn't drink every evening like other men. He listens to everything you say. You'll never get as faithful a man anywhere,' said Valli.

Valli dusted the floor of the verandah with her upper cloth and glanced at me.

'Why are you sitting here?' she asked me.

I sat down on the verandah near Valli. Valli held out a wad of betel leaves, lime paste and tobacco and said, 'Chew some betel leaves. You haven't eaten this morning, have you? Shall I give you some tea? There's tea on the boil.'

'No, I don't really want any. If you insist, I'll drink some, that's all,' murmured Maria, smiling.

Raghavan remarked, 'I heard someone say yesterday that his feet were hurting and he needed to drink some mutton soup.'

'Who said that, Raghava?'

'Someone who can't afford to buy a goat. I thought to myself then that a goat would be missing today . . .' said Prabhakaran.

'Dear God, how will I go back empty-handed to my family? I can't not go either. I have to give them something to eat. I ran out without even lighting the fire. Mary's father must be standing at the door, waiting for me,' said Maria. She spat the mixture of betel leaves and tobacco in her mouth into Valli's clean yard. And turned her eyes northward.

'I wonder whether Lasarappan saw my goat. Isn't that him, sitting on the grinding stone? Look carefully, Raghava.'

'That's not him. It's a crow that's come to eat funeral offerings. It's still early—Lasarappan wouldn't have woken up.'

'Let me go to that idiot-girl's house then and ask her. She's always sitting on the platform in front of the house, staring out. She's sure to have seen my goat,' said Maria, walking hurriedly northward. As soon as she arrived at the gate of Marar's house, she asked them something in a loud voice. Bala and I were just behind her but we could not make out what she was saying.

'Let's not follow her any more,' said Bala.

'Where can her goat be?' I asked.

'Maybe it's fallen into a well,' said Bala.

'Won't it die then?' I asked.

'Not necessarily. A black cat fell into our pond once. It lay there and mewed and mewed. It sank every now and then and came up again. Whenever it came up, it mewed. I called Amma. She took off her blouse and her mundu and jumped into the water. She was scared to catch the cat, since it was a wild one. Supposing it scratched her? Anyway, she finally reached out and caught it. When she brought it back, it scratched her twice on the cheek and fled! Evil creature! Amma still has the scars. The scratches took ages to heal. She used to apply a paste of raw turmeric and neem leaves to them every day—that was how they healed. Cat's claws are poisonous!' said Bala.

I saw Ammamma looking for me in the courtyard. So I went back to the Nalapat compound.

'Where were you, Kamala? Where did you go so early in the morning without even having breakfast?' she asked.

I scattered the flowers I had gathered in my skirt on the floor of the verandah. They looked beautiful against the floor smeared with cow dung.

'Won't Valiammaman be able to use these flowers for his puja?' I asked.

'Maybe. I don't know. He usually uses thechhi, pichakam and roses,' said Ammamma. She picked up the flowers, washed them and arranged them on a brass platter.

'Don't go near the fence to pluck flowers,' she said. 'There might be snakes there.'

'Tell her that again,' said Madhavi Amma. 'The child is always wandering around the western compound. She doesn't listen when I tell her. Not just snakes, there'll be crocodiles as well. Don't you know there are two crocodiles in the pond? I'm sure they come ashore now and then to bask in the sun. I saw one running over the grass one day with my own eyes! It went behind the outhouse, probably looking for some reptile to eat. What will you do if a crocodile winds itself around your leg? Tell the child how dangerous it is. There's no use crying after something terrible happens.'

'She's not afraid of anything because she lives in Calcutta. She doesn't even know snakes are poisonous! No one's explained these things to her either,' said Kali Narayanan.

'Let her grow up like that, not knowing fear,' said Ammamma.

'It's dangerous to grow up not knowing fear, Valiamma. The child will go with anyone who calls her. The other day she went off with the bangle seller Cherappan, across the field, right up to the carpenters' shed. Isn't that shameful? Is it right to give people reason to gossip? I called out to her loudly when I saw her and she came back. If I hadn't noticed and called her back, she'd have gone off with the fellow to the Poozhithala market! Disgraceful! And another day, I saw her walking behind the korathi, carrying the parrot's cage! It's all because no one here keeps her in check. What will we do if the korathi women carry her off? We'll have to look up at the sky and pray, that's all. Korathis live in the mountains—none of us will be able to get there,' said Narayanan Nair.

Ammamma's face suddenly reddened. She caught hold of my shoulders and stared into my eyes. Her tight grip hurt me. 'Kamala, never be so stupid again. What will people think if you go behind a bangle seller? Will you do that again?'

'No.'

'You mustn't go behind the korathi either.'

'I won't.'

'Come along then, dinner's ready. Unni has started to eat.'

While we were eating, Ettan said he was going to start a science magazine to teach ordinary people about new scientific discoveries.

'Who will write for it?' I asked.

'Marathattil Aniyan and I.'

'Are you both scientists?'

Looking annoyed, Ettan got up and went away. I had noticed that anything I said these days invariably annoyed him. The close bond we had shared during our childhood was slowly dissolving. I was never able to demonstrate the exceptional intelligence or capacity he expected of me.

'Will you tell Aami not to say silly things in front of my friends? She always insults me,' he told Ammamma one day.

'When did I insult you?' I asked, astonished.

'Didn't you ask me whether I was a scientist in front of Malathikutty? Doesn't that mean you don't believe I'm one?' Ettan asked.

'I didn't know you were one! That's why I asked,' I said, close to tears.

'Don't quarrel now. Anyway, Unni told you now that he's a scientist. You'd better believe him,' said Ammamma.

'What about me then? What am I? Just a girl?' I asked. I could feel my lips trembling.

'What science does Aami know . . .' muttered Ettan.

'So you think I have no brains at all?' I asked.

'Unni didn't say you have no brains,' said Ammamma.

'No one here likes me. I'm beginning to understand that. No matter what I do, everyone gets angry with me. It must be because I was born a girl that everyone has such contempt for me. I'm going away if no one wants me. I can earn my livelihood selling bangles. Or I'll buy a parrot and some cards and go around telling people's fortunes.'

Ettan laughed endlessly, hugging himself.

And at that moment, Ittiyachan's wife, Maria, went through our courtyard leading her goat.

'Where did you find it?' I called out to her.

'It was in the Palisserry folk's field, nibbling paddy. It's my good fortune no one caught it and made off with it.'

'You're right, your goat is a lucky creature. Did you see its udder? It's as big as a jackfruit!' said Kali Narayanan.

'Don't cast your evil eye on the creature, Kali. If the evil eye takes effect, my children will starve!'

'Oh, don't let your children starve because of my curse. I won't ever look at your goat again. Satisfied?' shouted Narayanan.

❖

My grandfather's younger brother, Chittanjoor Appu Thampuran, used to visit his sister-in-law, my grandmother, at least once in three months. His clothes, his hair and his teeth were all extraordinarily white. Although he was old, his voice was that of a young man. While he sat in the front room talking to Achan or Ammaman, he would sometimes speak in English. I would hover around, either in the same room or on the southern verandah, listening attentively while he spoke in the accents of an educated Englishman. Only later did someone tell me that Appu Thampuran taught English at the Zamorin's College in Calicut.

Leaning against a pillar in the front room, Appu Thampuran once said in English, 'I was unnerved.' The word 'unnerved' was unfamiliar to me then. It became my favourite word after this. Valiammaman, my older uncle, had acquired great scholarship in English by dint of his own efforts. But he did not have Appu Thampuran's purity of accent. He therefore spoke only in Malayalam to Malayali visitors.

Although his elder brother had been dead for many years, Appu Thampuran continued to show his elder brother's wife great respect. He always told her about his family problems and asked for her advice. Ammamma would stand behind the threshold of the thekkini and Appu Thampuran would stand leaning against a pillar in the southern verandah while these discussions took place. Appu Thampuran had never sat down in Ammamma's presence. Ammayi once remarked that Appu Thampuran conducted himself before Ammamma like Lakshmanan did when he went to see Sita. Laughing loudly, Ammaman retorted that Lakshmanan had never gone anywhere to see Sita, and that Appu Thampuran was like Hanuman when he met Sita in Lanka.

'Don't laugh like that—someone will hear,' said Ammayi.

Appu Thampuran had six children. He discussed the education of the sons and the marriage of the daughters with Ammamma in a low voice. The sincerity of his voice testified to the value he accorded to Ammamma's opinion. And this was what Ammamma appreciated and liked most: that others had such implicit faith in her.

Ammamma had eardrops or rings made out of my broken bangles or out of old earrings whose screws I had lost and gave them as wedding gifts to her husband's younger brother's daughters. According to custom, a widow was not allowed to visit the houses of her husband's relatives. It must have been because of this that Ammamma never participated in Appu Thampuran's children's wedding festivities. However, on the wedding day of each of the children, Ammamma usually talked about the celebrations to everyone at Nalapat and included a prathaman in the day's menu. Whenever she spoke about Thampuran or other members of the Chittanjoor family, Ammamma's voice would be full of affection. She did not have that kind of affection for anyone else.

'It's like you can gather honey from her mouth when she talks about the people of the kovilakam. Thampuran was her life. It's difficult to find two people who loved each other as much as they did. What if he was a Thampuran? He even used to have his dinner here. When he called out her name, Kochu, he barely said it fully,' said Unnimayamma. The old woman added that another couple who loved each other like Ammamma and her thampuran were Cheria Oppu and her husband, C.V. Subramania Iyer. 'Are there more like them?' I asked.

Unnimayamma leaned against the pillar and closed her eyes.

'Our Kunhan Nambisan and Brahmaniyamma,' she said. Then she smiled and added, 'Haven't you seen the old man who sits on the verandah of my house? You can count me and him too.'

'But there are so many others here who are married,' I said.

'All of them begin to fight with each other as soon as they're married.'

'Kutti Oppu and Ammaman don't quarrel,' I said.

Unnimayamma nodded and held up her index finger like a flag. 'That's true. They're like Shiva and Parvati. May God give them long life!'

'Do you know people who fight with each other, Unnimayamma?' I asked.

'Know? How many of them I've seen! The men get drunk by dusk. Then they go home at night and beat up the women and children and kick them. I tell you, child, at night you can hear the women screaming and crying and the men roaring like a velichappadu. Sometimes I even suspect they throw their little ones into the well.'

'Does your husband drink, Unnimayamma?' I asked.

'It's a sin to even suggest that, child. He sits on the verandah and says his prayers. He gives me no problems at all.'

Unnimayamma was a sumangali, a happily married woman, and the villagers considered it auspicious if they saw her as they set out on a journey. If anyone from the Ambazhathel family was going out, they'd arrange to have her stand at the gate. She wore a small golden pendant shaped like a temple bell on a string around her neck. She would stand at the gate with sandal paste marks on her forehead, neck and arms, her lips stained red with betel, ready to bring good fortune to everyone who passed by, especially Ambazhathel Kunhunni Ettan when he was going to Ponnani in connection with a court case. With Unnimayamma's death, fortune ceased to favour the Ambazhathel family and the property was divided. Cheria Oppu went away with her eldest son, Balettan, to the matam. And Kunhunni Ettan set out in a truck with his old cot, his steel trunks and his legal documents to his new house in Thrissur, his tears flowing copiously.

'This child loves listening to Unnimayamma's gossip,' remarked Madhavi Amma.

'You won't pass your exams if you sit listening to Unnimayamma's stories,' said Ammamma.

'Cheria Thampuratti is not like Unni Thampuran,' said Valli, laughing. 'They're very different. Unni Thampuran always has his nose in a book. But she likes to laugh. Once she finds something to laugh about, she doesn't bother about eating or sleeping.'

'She's not all that interested in studying,' said Ammamma. 'We should get her married before she turns fifteen.'

'Does everyone who's not interested in studying have to get married at fifteen?' I asked.

'What else can one do with them then? Keep them at home, doing nothing?' asked Ammamma.

'How old were you, Ammamma, when you were married?' I asked.

'I was married at thirteen. I was all of thirteen, running on fourteen. I had Bala when I was fifteen.'

'Can I have a baby at my age?' I asked. Madhavi Amma, Ammamma, Muthassi and Valli all burst out laughing.

'Don't be so foolish, Kamale,' said Ammamma. Even when she was angry, Ammamma's large eyes gleamed with affection for me.

Madhavi Amma said, 'You have to be fortunate, child, to marry early. It's not wealth that matters, or good looks. You have to have good fortune. They call it malayogam, the marriage destiny. There's a girl in my village from a very wealthy family. The jewellery she wears around her neck and on her hands and ears weighs all of thirty-eight sovereigns. She has a house and some land. A piece of land with a hundred and ten coconut palms on it. She's quite good-looking as well. Neither very fair nor very dark. What's the use? She's thirty-six now. Quite a number of

proposals came for her. Nothing turned out right. The
boy's family always said the girl was too educated. So
many boys came to see her. They would see the girl, eat
their fill of uppuma and steamed bananas, drink tea and
go their way. And after that a letter would arrive. Saying
that the girl was too educated.'

'To what level has she studied?' I asked.

'She's passed her tenth! All the boys who came had
failed in the seventh and stopped going to school. Who'll
marry girls who study too much? After all, boys don't tie
talis around girls' necks and take them into their families
to make teachers of them. What peace can there be in the
family if the girl takes the upper hand?' Madhavi Amma
asked this question of everyone in a loud voice.

'There's not a man around who's strong enough to make
you toe the line—that's why you're not married,' said Valli.
'Aren't you almost forty-five now?'

'What's wrong with you, Valli? What comfort does it
give you to add a few years to my age? You're always doing
that. All right then, add a few years more. Tell everyone
that I'm as old as you, Valli. You'll feel happier then.'
Madhavi Amma shrugged her shoulders.

'And what's wrong with you, Madhavi Amral? You've
never had a baby. So your body isn't damaged at all. Does
that mean you have to take a few years off your age?
Having a fair complexion doesn't mean you grow younger
every year, does it?' asked Valli.

'I know what you're suffering from, Valli. Jealousy! If
my body isn't damaged, it's because of the care I take of
it. Did anyone tell you not to take care of your body, Valli?
Get yourself some dasamoolarishtam to drink,' said
Madhavi Amma.

'Do you mean to say that if Valli drinks dasamoolarishtam, she'll become like Madhavi Amma?' asked Muthassi.

'Will I become as fair as you, Madhavi Amral, if I take dasamoolarishtam?' asked Valli.

'Can a crow turn into a stork if it has a bath?' Narayanan Nair's voice floated out from the kitchen. Even the simple-minded young girl who worked for us laughed at the question. Spiced vegetable wafers lay drying on mats spread in the courtyard and the girl's work was to shout 'Go, go!' and shoo away the crows that crowded on to them. She was given the previous day's kanji for breakfast in the morning and lunch at noon as wages. Sometimes in the afternoons, when Ammamma and the others were asleep, she would push my swing for me. Ammamma did not like my touching her.

'Play all you want with her, but don't touch her,' Ammamma would say to me. I ignored this command. It may have been because I was growing up in Calcutta that I did not believe in differences of caste and creed. Not wishing to hurt Ammamma, however, I always tried to avoid bringing subjects of this nature into our conversation.

❖

'It was only after I set out that I remembered that it was an inauspicious hour. So I went back home again and spent some time with Amma. You can't go and see a newborn baby during the inauspicious pattu rashi period, you know!' said Ammu Amma to everyone in general, as she came into the Nalapat compound. She had come to see my Cheriamma's first baby. She wore a loose, striped blouse and a shining white mundu and veshti. A smile lit up her fair face from time to time. No one in her family came much to Nalapat. When Cheriamma married

Thendiyath Appunni Menon, we acquired a number of new relatives.

Ammamma was overjoyed to see her. She rushed up, her cheeks flushed, and led Ammu Amma to the middle room upstairs where Cheriamma lay. Unnimayamma was seated on the floor with the baby on her lap. Ammu Amma screwed up her eyes and looked hard at the child, then took out a crumpled rupee note tucked into her waist and handed it to Unnimayamma, who touched it to her eyes.

'Don't you want to carry the baby?' asked the old woman.

'No. Let it sleep peacefully. If I handle it and it wakes up, it might start to cry,' said Ammu Amma, smiling.

'It was a quick delivery,' said Ammamma. 'I was quite worried. Rather late in life, and her first . . . but there were no problems at all.'

'There wasn't much delay, then?' asked Ammu Amma.

'No, it was all over very quickly.'

'The spitting image of the father!'

Cheriamma smiled. She peered at the locket on her chain as if to sharpen her memory—there was a picture of Appunni Ettan on it. Ammu Amma laughed loudly and leaned over to examine the locket.

'Sundari wears a locket around her neck as well. Is it the fashion now to wear lockets with one's husband's picture?'

Cheriamma was silent. She just kept smiling. Ammu Amma placed the little paper packet she had brought on the bed.

'I don't know whether you'll like the colour. It's a piece of cloth to make a dress for the baby. If you think it's not suitable, make a blouse for Amma with it. It's a colour that will suit either of them.' She laughed loudly, certain she had said something amusing.

Ammamma opened the packet and took out the piece of cloth. It was white with pale blue dots.

'It's first class fabric,' said Ammamma.

'Amma asked me not to buy green or red. We prefer light shades.'

'Me too,' said Cheriamma. 'I don't like dark shades.'

'You'll look good in red,' said Unnimayamma.

'It's a colour only Chettiar women wear! They wear bright red and green saris,' said Ammamma.

'Have you seen Thiya women? Have you seen the saris they wear when they're going to Kaplingattu or for a wedding? They wear only dark colours. As far as the colours of clothes go, they outdo Chettiar women these days!' said Ammu Amma.

'You'd mistake them for Nair women except for the colour of their saris. And their jewels are all pure gold, aren't they? It's Nairs who are suffering under the evil influence of Saturn these days!' Ammamma's laughter echoed Ammu Amma's.

'Did you see the little pendant around my neck? It weighs five fanams. My children will take care of me as long as it lies around my neck, I'm sure of that,' said Unnimayamma.

'Are you saying then that your children will not take care of you if it's not there?' asked Ammu Amma.

'I'm not talking only of my children—I'm talking of all the children born in this world,' said Unnimayamma. 'They'll look after their mothers as long as they're sure of getting some money out of them. If there's no money to be had, they don't want their mothers!'

'You're just making that up, Unnimayamma. Your children really look after you well. It's a sin to talk about them like that.'

'Only God and I know what's happening with me,' muttered the old woman.

'Can you sow beans and reap gram? You get only what you give. If you love your children, they'll love you in return,' said Ammu Amma.

'You can sow beans but they won't sprout unless they are destined to. Don't you know that? What if stray cattle come and eat up the beans as they sprout?' asked Unnimayamma.

'The old woman's cornered me there!' said Ammu Amma, smiling. She noticed me, for the first time.

'So you're here, sitting so quietly! Do you want to hold Cheriamma's baby? What are you going to call her?'

'Appunni Menon said we'd name her Vasanthi,' said Ammamma.

'Vasanthi—that's an excellent name,' said Ammu Amma.

'There's a Vasanthi in the poet Vallathol's family,' said Ammamma.

'How old is Kamala now? She was a little girl when she came for the temple festival in Punnukkavu the year before the last. She's grown so much!'

'Girls grow up fast at this age. We'll have to start looking for a husband for her in another two years!' said Ammamma.

'Poor child, she's such a little thing! She's not old enough to get married. Let her study and put on some weight. None of you eat meat, do you? So you'll have to give her plenty of milk. And roasted bananas are very healthy. Our Prabha wouldn't put on any weight until I gave him roasted bananas. He has rounded out well now. Give her a lot of milk and two vadas made of urad dal before she goes to bed at night. She'll fill out in no time.'

'That's easy. We can make urad dal vadas for tea and put aside a couple for her to eat at night. I'll try that on Kamala,' said Ammamma.

'Boil some navara rice in milk and rub it over her body—the child's skin will grow fairer. You have to make sure girls have a good complexion. It's not enough for them to be rounded. Smear oil over her limbs, then grind raw turmeric and rub it into the skin. It's very good. And add kurunthotti to the milk in which the navara rice is boiled. If you do all this for twenty-one days, her skin will take on the colour of gold,' said Ammu Amma.

'Twenty-one days! I can't keep her here even a week. They'll be off to Calcutta by the time her school reopens. And you can't get these things in Calcutta!' lamented Ammamma.

'I'm sure the Bengalis boil milk with kurunthotti in it and rub it over their bodies. It's just that we don't know about the things they do. Women don't tell the whole world about the measures they take to be healthy and beautiful. They are family secrets.'

'I wonder from where you got your wonderful complexion,' mused Unnimayamma in an undertone.

Ammu Amma laughed. 'I had it when I was born. Haven't you seen my mother? I inherited her complexion. I've never had the need to rub kurunthotti or navara into my skin!'

Overcome by a feeling of inferiority, I hastily left the room, my head lowered. Marathu Radha was in the thekkini downstairs, leaning against the pillar. God had given her the same brown-toned skin that I had.

'Come on, Radha, let's get some raw turmeric and rub it on our bodies.'

'Whatever for?' asked Radha.

'So that we can become fair!' I said.

Radha nodded. There were two turmeric plants growing in the courtyard of our nalukettu. I pulled out one with an effort. We washed it and ground it on a stone. My fingers were stained a dazzling yellow. I rubbed the paste over my face and arms and legs. Radha smeared it only over her face.

Madhavi Amma came that way and flew into a temper. 'Are you trying to dress up like mookolachathans?' she asked.

'Don't speak to her,' I whispered in Radha's ear. Radha closed her eyes, stretched out her legs and sat immobile.

'Are you going for the festival in the Pavittamkulangara temple?' asked Madhavi Amma.

'We're not going anywhere,' I said angrily.

'Don't go out with turmeric smeared all over you. People will scold you. It's Ammini Amma who's just had a baby and here you are, running around with turmeric on you!' Madhavi Amma laughed derisively.

Radha smiled. Like me, she had fine hair on her arms. I examined her arms.

'I know a way of removing this hair,' I said.

'What's that?' she asked.

'You know the woman who looks after me in Calcutta, Tripura? She told me what to do. You have to smear hot ash from the fireplace over your hands and legs and pluck out the hair. It will never grow again. Let's go to the kitchen . . .'

'It's sure to hurt,' said Radha.

'So what? We'll look so beautiful when the hair is gone. Then we'll put on saris and look really good . . .'

'Kali Narayanan Nair won't let us into the kitchen,' said Radha.

'We'll go while he's asleep.'

'Why go to all that trouble, children? Wear long skirts if you have hair on your legs. Why burn yourself with hot ash?' asked Madhavi Amma.

'I don't have long skirts,' I said.

'Ask your parents to get a couple made. Tell your father you're fed up with baby clothes. Tell him you can't go around showing your knees any longer.'

Ammamma and Ammu Amma came down the stairs just then.

'Go off to the vadikkini, children,' said Madhavi Amma. We scrambled hurriedly to our feet. Radha tried to hide behind the pillar.

'What on earth has the child smeared on her face?' asked Ammu Amma.

'What is it? Turmeric? Why have you rubbed turmeric all over yourself at this time of day?' asked Ammamma. I didn't dare answer.

❖

The Nalapat folk used to buy curd and ghee for birthday feasts and other festivals from Mullathel Raman Nair. He arrived one day in the portico on the south to collect the money they owed him and cleared his throat many times to catch someone's attention. He even spat noisily into the yard once or twice. Finally he called out loudly, 'Isn't there anyone here?' Then he went down the steps and skirted the house all the way round until he reached the portico on the north. His ankles showed below his thin mundu.

It was four o'clock. The evening sunlight that fell over the pomegranate and mango trees dazzled Raman Nair's eyes. He had ash-coloured pupils. He was completely free of the evil-mindedness that was a trait in the wealthy people of Punnayoorkulam.

The servants were discussing a wedding that had recently taken place in the village. One of them asked Raman Nair for his opinion and he spat out again, slowly and dramatically.

'If beauty is a consideration,' he said, 'no one can compare with the girls in our village. Not even if you go to the Vadakkunannathan temple in Thrissur will you see girls with such grace. And yet the people here go looking for buck-toothed girls in some faraway village! I can't understand why. Ghouls that are not worthy enough even to lick the feet of our girls. Maybe they think girls who hang lots of gold around their necks don't need to be graceful or beautiful. After all, some of our girls here can afford only a black thread around their neck and a little pendant on it. But that's more than enough. Our girls are like celestial maidens!'

'Indeed! True, they may have fair skins, full breasts and long, thick hair. But those who have no money can't afford to look after their bodies. So as time passes, their skins darken, their breasts grow flat and pendulous and their hair begins to thin out. Only women from wealthy families really maintain their beauty,' said Kali Narayanan Nair with a deep sigh.

'Do you mean to say that the girls here should be given to rich men from other places? Are you suggesting that we give them off to wealthy Chettiars from Coimbatore?' Raman Nair arched his back like a bow in an excess of emotion. The towel that lay on his left shoulder slid to the ground.

'So you're going to wait, are you, for Chettiars to turn up from Coimbatore? They can get first class Chettichi girls from their own place, dark maybe, but really good-looking. I've seen a lot of them in Pazhani. Their lips are the colour of jnaval fruit. Black is beautiful too, haven't you heard, Raman Nair?' asked Kali Narayanan, breaking a coconut with grave deliberation.

Madhavi Amma, busy chopping yam in neat cubes for kalan and arranging them on an enamel platter, looked at him from the corner of her eyes.

'*You* won't have any problem getting your girls married. They've all got your complexion. There are so many young men just waiting to get fair girls. They're difficult to find these days, I'm told. All the girls go to school now. They walk miles in the sun and their skins grow dark and tanned. Girls never went out in the olden days. They used to have regular oil baths and stay home. That's why their skins had that special glow. You'll never see such girls again, not even if you perform penance!' said Madhavi Amma.

'It's not right to say that everyone who goes to school turns dark. Don't my children go to school? And what happened—did they grow dark? No, they didn't! Have you seen my daughter, Janu? She's the colour of pure gold! Radiant!' exclaimed Raman Nair.

'I've seen her. She's fair all right. But the girl has your light eyes,' said Madhavi Amma.

'What's so surprising about that? What's wrong if she has her father's looks? That's a fine thing to say!' Raman Nair wiped his face with a towel.

'All I said was that she has light eyes. I didn't say it's wrong to have them!' said Madhavi Amma.

'The breeze wafting through our coconut palms here makes our girls' skins turn fair. But once they're married and taken away from here, our girls become dark. Just look at Balamani Amma. Hasn't she become thin and sunburnt after going to Calcutta? And you know Ambazhathel Kamala's daughter, Leela. Palisserry Pappi Amma's son, Govindankutty, married her and took her away to Ananthapuram. When she came back a year later, no one could recognize the girl—her skin had turned so dark! She wore a bright red sari, the colour Chettichis wear and she'd stuck a whole lot of leaves and plants into her hair! And the other one, Kannathu Kalyani Amma's

daughter. That one's forgotten how to speak Malayalam—
she speaks only Tamil now!'

Raman Nair leaned against a pillar, evidently needing
its support. 'You're right. Those who leave this place
become dark. Look at all those who've always stayed here.
Haven't you seen the lady of Ambazhathel? And the Valia
Thamburatti of Eliyangode? Even at this age, their cheeks
have the flush of youth . . .' said Madhavi Amma.

'If you want to see someone with really fair skin, you
must go to Palisserry. Have you seen Pappi Amma? She
has skin the colour of milk that's been simmering over the
fire till it's thick and creamy. And the grandmother—her
skin is pristine white! And Lakshmikutty Amma, Kalathingal
Kuttappa Menon's wife—she has glowing skin too. But
her children haven't inherited it,' said Narayanan Nair.

Raman Nair said suddenly, 'Look, I've been waiting
here for ages. Go and call Kochu Amma. I need that money
today. I have to give in my contribution to the chit fund.'

I was sitting on the steps leading from the vadikkini to
the verandah outside. He looked at me and smiled. 'Have
you been sitting here listening to the funny things adults
say, child? Go and call Ammamma.'

'She's gone to Ambazhathel,' I said.

'Oh yes, I forgot to tell you. Balakrishna Menon's wife,
Sundari, has gone into labour,' said Madhavi Amma.

'When?' asked Raman Nair.

'Early morning. She didn't tell anyone. She went off
for a bath and the water broke. So they sent for the nurse,'
said Madhavi Amma.

'Then there's no point my waiting here. By the time
she has had the baby, it will be late evening. She may not
even deliver today—it could be tomorrow. What will I do
now? I need the money urgently. I have to pay for the chit

fund. But it's not right to go to Ambazhathel and ask Kochu Amma for money now.'

'No, it isn't. Wait until the baby is born. Your chit fund can wait,' said Narayanan Nair.

'People who run a chit fund won't wait for babies to be born! Let me see if I can get the money elsewhere,' said Raman Nair.

'How much do you need?' asked Madhavi Amma.

'Why, do you have money to lend me?'

'Maybe I do. How much do you want? You can give it back to me tomorrow.'

'Six and a half rupees, that's all.'

'I'll get it for you—let me wash my hands first. They're itching because I've been cleaning yam.' Madhavi Amma got up and went to the vadikkini.

'She's saving money to buy herself a necklace set with red stones,' said Narayanan Nair.

'She's already made bangles and a pair of earrings. That's smartness for you! Women should be smart enough to get themselves enough gold to wear. Once they have gold, men will come looking for them. And marry them. If she doesn't have gold, she'll never get a man at her age,' said Raman Nair.

When Raman Nair had gone, Madhavi Amma said, 'He's a well-bred person.'

'It's an old family, the Mullathel taravad.'

Mambulli Krishnan's wife rushed up just then. 'Sundari Thamburatti's baby's come . . . a boy.'

'So that's over. Now whoever went from here can come back,' said Kali Narayanan Nair mockingly.

'In any case, why should anyone go running from here if someone at Ambazhathel is having a baby?' asked Madhavi Amma agitatedly. 'That's a midwife's work!'

'Careful, the child's listening,' said Narayanan Nair.

'Let her listen! I said what I thought, that's all. I don't like the idea of people going from here to attend on childbirths. I feel ashamed!' said Madhavi Amma, deliberately raising her voice.

'But they're relatives, aren't they? If they send word that labour's begun, someone has to go from here. It's only courtesy,' said Narayanan Nair.

'Not where I come from. Only midwives go for childbirths. Sometimes a washerwoman goes along too. No one else ever goes,' said Madhavi Amma.

'The child will carry all this to Valiamma now. And you'll be scolded. Why talk of such things? Which of us is rich? None of us have any money. The family gives us five or ten rupees, and we slave to get that. Whatever we pretend we are, none of us is really worth a paisa. How many servants have come and gone in this place! Who remembers any of them now? It's only as long as we stay here that we can claim to have some kind of dignity. Don't forget that, Madhavi Amma,' said Kali. He struck a coconut against the edge of the grinding stone and broke it into two. He poured the water that dribbled out into his mouth. Licking his lower lip with relish, he smiled at me.

'Do you want water from a coconut?' he asked.

'Yes, I do,' I said.

'I can't give you any today. Tomorrow morning when I break a coconut, I'll keep aside the water in a cup for you, child. All right?'

❖

It was the custom at Nalapat house to set out a number of auspicious objects on a low, tortoise-shaped wooden stool from the first day of Karkatakam for four full weeks. The stool would be placed on the northern side of the door of the machu and on it would be arranged the ten flowers sacred to that month, sandal paste, kajal, theertham and arichandu. They were meant for the goddess Sri Bhagavathi so that she would come and bless the house.

Muthassi asked the women servants the previous day whether they had plucked all the flowers we needed. Many medicinal plants grew in the southern compound between the coconut palms that had been planted in memory of the dead who were cremated there. If a wasp or a scorpion or a centipede were to sting you, you had only to pluck the adambu creeper growing on the fence, wring out the juice from it and rub it on the sting for the pain to subside like magic.

The women servants knew how to identify the different plants. They would pluck out the plants they needed by the roots, wash them well and wrap them in banana leaves to keep them fresh.

Every morning in Karkatakam, the women of the house, particularly the unmarried girls and married women, would have a bath, go up to the machu and apply the kajal kept on the stool there to their eyes. Then they would place the arichandu on their foreheads to form a round pottu, wind the ten auspicious flowers into their hair and partake of the theertham in which tulasi leaves had been soaked.

The Nalapat women did not generally use kajal or perfume or wear flowers in their hair. They did not want to be known as lovers of luxury and took great care to be simply dressed. But I had inherited my father's complexion and looks and was very different from all of them. Which might have been why I learned how to apply kajal to my eyes regularly from the servant women and put on a pottu.

When I came to the village for my holidays, I would send for the bangle seller and buy glass bangles to wear.

I once asked Ammamma loudly, 'Why is no one here wearing glass bangles or kajal in their eyes?'

'Only Mohiniyattam dancers dress up like that. Those who stay at home don't have to,' muttered Ammamma.

'But shouldn't people feel happy when they look at us? Shouldn't they think we're beautiful?' I asked.

'And what use would it be if they thought you were?' countered Ammamma.

'Isn't beauty useful in any way?' I did not mean that question for anyone in particular. But Muthassi heard it. She continued to say her prayers, the chain of tulasi beads in her hand moving fast as she kept count.

'And what use is it to say prayers?' I asked loudly.

Muthassi continued to pray, 'Namah Shivaya . . . Namah Shivaya.'

'Are you saying your prayers to please Shiva?' I asked.

'Kamala, go and read something,' said Ammamma. Dismissing me from the scene was a trick she often resorted to when she was defeated in argument.

I wandered into the vadikkini where a group of women were seated around a soot-covered chimney lamp.

'Why don't Amma and Ammamma apply kajal in their eyes?' I asked Madhavi Amma.

'Their eyes are very beautiful even without kajal, child. Women who have chinky eyes or a squint have to use kajal. Otherwise they'd be really ugly.'

'Am I cross-eyed?' I asked.

'Not that I can see. And you don't have chinky eyes either.'

'Then why is it that I apply kajal?'

'Don't do it then—don't be the only one in your family to do it. I heard Valiamma say the other day that the women of this family don't wear nose rings either. Every family has its own rules. Don't break them, child.'

'Is everyone in your family allowed to wear kajal, Madhavi Amma? And nose rings?'

'Oh yes, they can wear kajal and nose rings. And flowers in their hair too. Look at my earrings. Sankaranarayanan had them made for me. They're as big as old-fashioned thodas. They're filled with lac inside, but who would know that? Would your mother ever wear earrings like these? No, she wouldn't. That's why I said every family makes its own rules,' said Madhavi Amma.

'If only I had been born in your family, Madhavi Amma!'

She laughed. 'There's nothing wrong with the family you've been born in. You have excellent parents. Sometimes I even think they're a little too good for the people here. Human beings shouldn't be too good. Do you know why? Evil people will have no respect for them. They'll think, "These good people, they'll never betray us, or take revenge on us. So let's deceive them." That's why I say don't be too good, child. You must be capable of looking after your own affairs. You must demand the money people owe you,' said Madhavi Amma.

'Whose money are you talking about?'

'Haven't you seen the people who come and flatter your father, treating him with exaggerated respect? Do you think they're really sincere? They're not. They're cheats. They put on a show to get money out of him. They know how vulnerable he is. What a lot of money your father gives them! It's true he works in Calcutta and earns well. But money doesn't grow on trees in Calcutta. These greedy creatures would pretend they didn't know your father if he had no money. V.M. Nair? Which V.M. Nair? We don't know anyone like that, that's what they'd say. You don't understand, child. If you did, wouldn't you tell your father not to throw money at everyone who comes? In the end, he'll have no more money to give. And at that point, you can comb the whole village and you won't find a single one of these flatterers anywhere!'

'You don't like anyone in our village, do you, Madhavi Amma?' I asked.

Madhavi Amma raised the wick of the lamp and laughed mirthlessly.

'I'm not attached to anyone, nor do I bear anyone rancour. After all, it's not my money that's going. But take care of yourself, child. It's the money that's meant to educate you, make you a doctor, get you married that these tricksters are taking away. You'll never see it again. Your father lives in Calcutta. People who live there are not like those who live here—they're good-hearted. Which is why your father can't make out that these people are deceiving him. If someone comes asking for two rupees, does he have to give them five? If he's got a hoard stashed away in his box, can't he use it to have jewels made for Balamani Amma?'

'What are you talking about? Do you really think Balamani Amma will go around wearing chains and bangles like you?' asked Meenakshikutty.

'Why, isn't she young? And isn't her husband alive? Why does she have to make herself look like an old widow?'

'Shut up, Madhavi Amma. The child will go and repeat all this to Valiamma. And Valiamma won't like it, you know that.'

'The child tell her? She doesn't carry tales. She doesn't know how to gossip and make mischief. Maybe she'll learn all that when she grows older. But she doesn't do things like that now.'

'Yes, because she goes to school with Bengalis. Once she moves here, she'll rot. She'll learn how to tell tales and betray friends and all that. Two years of staying here and she'll be another person. This is an evil place. If someone were to come and invite me to go away with them, I'd pack my things that minute and go. And never come back!'

'You're young, Meenakshikutty. You're sure to get married. And it's a long time since your man died. But what if some widower comes asking for you? There are widowers who want to get married again because there's no one to look after their children. There are Tamil widowers who come here looking for wives. They think the world of Malayali women. Their own women are quite worthless—their skins are as black as soot! Of course they say black can be beautiful too. But I've never been able to appreciate that. The radiance of our women . . . it's something quite unique! Not just Nair women but all the other castes as well. That Veluthedathu Lakshmikutty's daughter, for instance: she looks like a princess! And now that it's Karkatakam, Lakshmikutty will give her mukuttu oil to rub on her body and neelibringhadi oil for her hair. She'll break a raw egg into her mouth and wash it down with a ladleful of sesame oil. And the girl will look ravishing. It isn't the girl you've seen in Midhunam, the month before Karkatakam, that you'll see in Chingam, the month after. It's the medicines you take in Karkatakam that really invigorate the body. Nothing you take during the other months will ever be as effective.'

'And what medicine are you taking this month, Madhavi Amma?' asked Meenakshikutty.

'If I do take something, I won't go telling the whole world about it, Meenakshikutty. Medicines have to be taken in secret, or they won't have any effect.'

'If I knew what it was, I could take it too and improve my health.'

'Your body doesn't lack anything, Meenakshikutty. If you take medicines when you don't need them, your body won't be able to endure their heat. I've seen people becoming weak and thin with the medicines they take and their bodies growing shrivelled. Take care, don't take any kind of medicinal lehyam unless you really need it.'

'It's not that I don't want to take lehyams. I can't afford them. I bought two red-bordered mundus and two mull mundus with last month's salary. I still owe Chetty, the cloth vendor, three and a half rupees. Do you owe him anything?'

'I never take anything on credit, Meenakshikutty. I don't like to strut around in clothes I've not paid for. How many times that Perumal Chetty tried to foist his wares on me! He'd make a long speech to convince me that I'd look good in a green-bordered mundu. But I can't bear to buy on credit. I want to be sure I don't owe anyone anything when I die.'

'You're not going to die so soon, Madhavi Amma. You'll be alive when all of us die. Looking at you, your build and your complexion, I can tell you'll live another thirty years!'

'Don't cast the evil eye on me—I'm very susceptible. Someone just has to say I have a glowing complexion and I immediately start a headache. And a throbbing pain in my bones. The only way I can find relief is to ask Amina Umma to come and exorcise the evil eye.'

'So one has to suffer if one is beautiful, isn't that right, Madhavi Amma? It's the ugly ones who are lucky. They're never affected by the evil eye!' declared Meenakshikutty.

'In that case, Thoniyare Paru Amma is a lucky woman, isn't she?' I asked.

'Of course! She's really fortunate. The money she makes! She gets thirty rupees for each person with smallpox that she nurses.'

'I'd die of fear if I so much as saw a person with smallpox!'

'And what if you caught it yourself, Meenakshikutty?' asked Madhavi Amma.

'Don't ever say that. It terrifies me even to hear it said! Don't talk about things like that at this twilight hour, Madhavi Amma.'

'It's the hour when Bhagavathi comes out to walk around. Sometimes you can hear her anklets tinkling in the courtyard . . .'

'Shh . . . the child will get frightened.'

'I'm not frightened of anyone!' I said.

'Go and read for a while, child, or you'll be scolded for sitting here too long,' said Meenakshikutty.

Ammamma took off the glasses balanced on the tip of her nose as I walked into the thekkini and asked, 'Was Madhavi telling you stories?'

'No,' I answered, 'she wasn't.'

'You've grown up now, Kamala. You don't have to listen to her stories. You can read books. Isn't that much more enjoyable?'

'I will,' I said.

'Go and take an English book from the front room,' said Ammamma. 'Will you read it to us and explain what it means?'

I took out the novel *Manon Lescaut* from Ammaman's bookshelf and placed it in front of the big brass oil lamp. The figure of a woman was drawn on its red leather jacket in gold lines.

'Read, Kamala,' said Ammamma.

I did not have the patience to read out a whole love story to them. When I had read half a page, I closed the book and yawned.

'You prefer the children's *Mahabharatam*, don't you, Kamala?' asked Ammamma.

'Don't read now, in this light. It's not good for your eyes,' said Muthassi.

'Her vision is bad enough as it is. She needs glasses to read. What a pity she has to wear glasses at her age!' said Ammamma. The compassion in her voice brought tears to my eyes. I lay down on Ammamma's lap and listened to Muthassi chanting Namah Shivaya . . .

The clock in the room announced that it was eight.

❖

One day, at about four o'clock in the evening, a strange, twisted figure appeared under the mango tree in the western yard. I had just had tea and come out to the portico. The figure stared at me and I was frightened. I had no idea who he was or why he had come. His eyes were fixed on the emptiness that hung above the fields beyond the gate. He wore an old coat and his face was covered with grey stubble. In his right hand, he clutched a bent cane stick.

'Who is it?' I asked loudly. He pretended he had not heard me. I went in and called Madhavi Amma to the portico.

'Did he frighten you, child? That's our Raman,' said Madhavi Amma. My anxious look amused her. Raman did not say anything.

'What is it, Rama?' she asked.

'I wanted to see the master from Calcutta,' he said.

'He's gone to Guruvayoor. To Vadekkara. We've no idea when he'll be back. He might stay there tonight, worship in the temple tomorrow and then get back.'

'I'll wait here,' growled Raman.

'How long are you going to wait? You'd better go away now and come back tomorrow evening,' said Madhavi Amma. Raman continued to stand there like an abandoned statue.

'You want to ask him for money, don't you? I've been noticing that everyone who comes here borrows money before they go back. But they never return it. That's the way they behave in this village. Master comes for three weeks, wanting to sit back on his couch and relax and they arrive one by one, grinning foolishly, determined to get money out of him. They have to get someone treated in the hospital, get their girls married, conduct a sixteenth-day ceremony for a relative who died, buy a cow: that's what they say. And they go away with a stack of rupee notes!' Madhavi Amma spoke in a loud voice. Raman was silent. He lowered the bent tip of his stick into the sand and rested his chin on it.

'The children are scared of you. Go away now and come tomorrow evening,' repeated Madhavi Amma.

Raman did not move. I went in and sat at the edge of the courtyard in the nalukettu.

'Why are you so frightened of him, child?' asked Madhavi Amma.

'I'm not frightened,' I said.

'Just don't go near him. He's ill—some incurable disease.'

Raman coughed. A cough full of phlegm.

'Incurable?' I asked.

'Yes, child. God gives people incurable diseases as punishment for the sins they committed in a previous life,' said Madhavi Amma. 'There's no use treating them.'

'What did Raman do in his previous life?' I asked, feeling very uneasy.

'How do we know? Only God knows such things.'

'If I commit sins in this life, will I fall ill in my next life?' I asked.

'Of course! If you commit a sin, you have to endure its consequences,' said Madhavi Amma. Dusk had fallen, Jupiter had risen in the south-western corner of the sky and Raman still waited under the mango tree for Achan to arrive, as obstinate as the fear that lurked in my mind of committing some grave sin . . .

When I went to bed that night, I spoke to Ammamma about Raman's incurable disease.

'There's nothing wrong with him, I'm sure of that. Madhavi is just making it up,' she said.

'Have you seen anyone with an incurable disease?' I asked.

'No,' said Ammamma.

'There's no one in the village who suffers from one?' I asked.

'No. People get colds and fevers. Or eczema or something like that. A touch of rheumatism when they grow old. I've not seen any other disease here.'

'Then why do people here die if they don't have terrible illnesses?' I asked.

'People die when it's time for them to go. They don't need to fall ill before they die.'

She explained to me that many people at Nalapat had died without having been victims of a long illness. People who were going to die could often foresee their death. They would observe a fast on Ekadashi and on the next day, Dwadashi, they would have a bath, partake of theertham from the temple and lie down to die, their minds at peace. For most people at Nalapat, death seemed to have been a pleasant experience.

After Ammamma told me all this, I used to grow uneasy every time I saw Ekadashi marked on the calendar. I would be afraid that one of my relatives would be preparing to die on Dwadashi.

I told Madhavi Amma once, 'If Ammamma dies, I'll die at once too.' Madhavi Amma laughed.

'The child adores her Ammamma! Listen child, if you get married and have a baby, will you love Ammamma as much as you love the baby? You won't! You'll love Ammamma only as long as you don't have a husband and child of your own. Ammamma won't matter to you after that!' Tears streamed from my eyes. I could not bear to think of a time when I would no longer love Ammamma. It was her love that nourished my life. And yet there were so many occasions when I ignored her and spent time with my friends.

'It's difficult to see Kamala alone now—she's always surrounded by friends,' Ammamma would say. Seated on the steps of Ambazhathel, singing songs and talking to my friends, I would feel hurt when she said that. But I no longer found time to be alone with her; I was with them all the time. And the subjects we discussed would not have pleased Ammamma. We spoke eagerly about boys and love. I had become fed up with hearing about the subjects Ammamma favoured: Mahatma Gandhi, the spiritual life and so on. I was more interested in talking about fashionable clothes and the good looks of film actors. Learning about Ramakrishna Paramahamsa or listening to the verses Vivekananda had composed bored me. I became convinced during that period that I was just an ordinary girl and very different from the Nalapat folk, although I had been born in their family. And I made no effort to turn my thoughts to spiritual things. A healthy body and the first suggestions of beauty I saw made me arrogant. It may have been because I grew up in Calcutta that the tunes of

Bengali love songs thudded like waves ceaselessly upon my ears. I experienced a singular longing to leave childhood behind and be transformed into a woman. I wanted to smear red sindooram on my forehead and in the parting of my hair, wear shell bangles and redden my feet with alta. In the cold season, I rubbed mustard oil on my body before a bath, just as Bengalis did, and afterwards I left my waist-length hair unbound.

One day, Ammaman, who was lying on the easy chair in the front room, overheard a story I was telling Malathikutty, one of Bankim Chandra Chatterjee's. He sent for me later and praised my style of narration. He said I had acquired my skill in storytelling from Bengal. He told me that I should consider it my great good fortune to be able to live as a Bengali and a Malayali at the same time.

Ammaman never failed to tell us children how proud he was of our achievements. It gave him no pleasure at all to listen to reports of the cleverness of children who did not belong to Nalapat. He would say, 'They are just ordinary children! How much can you expect from them?' It was Ammaman who first made me conscious of the importance of nurturing my individuality. My teachers in Calcutta had counselled me to try to merge with the crowd and suppress my own individuality. They had encouraged me through their words and actions to cloak my body, my heart and my thoughts in the uniform of ordinariness, which they said would simultaneously become my clothing and my armour.

The teacher who gave me private lessons in mathematics once asked me, 'Kamala, why do you take delight in always doing something different? Can't you behave like everyone else? Do you want to make yourself conspicuous?'

I was taken aback. I put my head down on the table and wept. I felt that those who were dear to me considered whatever I did or did not do either a fault or foolishness.

But at Nalapat, in front of Ammaman, I never had to despise myself or feel inferior. In his infinite kindness, this philosopher wanted me to develop a sense of superiority that might have been illusory but that nourished my spirit. Even Ammamma did not have the courage to reprimand me in his presence.

Poor Ammamma! She was afraid that I would grow into a coquette because every time I came home for the holidays, I wore fragrant flowers in my hair, tinkling glass bangles on my hands and smeared my palms with henna. I carried around with me a picture as my constant companion: a portrait of the poet Lord Byron. He stood proudly with a black cape over his shoulders and thick, wavy hair. I used to hang the picture in my bedroom in a spot where I would see it as soon as I woke up. Although I had told Ammamma a hundred times that he was dead, she had grave suspicions about him. What if that poet, whose religion was different from ours, arrived in Calcutta and led me astray?

Muthassi, calm and unruffled by nature, saw things differently. 'He's quite good-looking. He's untied his tuft, hasn't he? But look . . . isn't he a Christian?' she asked. She hated to hurt anyone.

'Aren't Bala and Madhavan Nair unhappy about this?' she asked me in a low voice.

'Why? Why should they be unhappy if I keep this picture in my room?'

'It's not the picture that will displease them. But if you marry a Christian, Kamala . . .'

I told Muthassi over and over again that Byron was dead.

'No one sits gazing at a dead man's picture, I'm sure of that. You're not such a fool, Kamala,' she insisted.

Ammamma, who was combing my hair, answered her, 'You have no idea, Amma. Kamala is utterly stupid! I sometimes feel when I see her do things like this that she's completely mad!' I turned around and caught her smiling. Her pale face and that smile still linger in my memory.

❖

In those days, there used to be a Chinaman who went from house to house in Calcutta selling dresses and lace-edged slips. Maybe there was more than one, but they looked the same to me. All of us children addressed him as 'Chinaman'. He didn't really bother to show children any special affection. Afraid that our muddy hands would stain his goods, he would follow our every move closely with his eyes.

When he opened his khaki bundle on the wooden ledge in our front verandah, everyone's eyes would light up with wonder. He would unfurl rolls of silk that had the colour of butter and the softness of a bird's wing. We would touch with admiration petticoats and chemises edged with lace the colour of tea leaves. All the clothes had the same fragrance: the scent of camellia flowers. I would visualize exquisitely beautiful women walking slowly, wearing such clothes. I felt that wearing clothes like those was like wearing beauty itself. But, unfortunately, they were all clothes made for adults.

'Don't you have clothes for children?' Amma asked the Chinaman.

'We don't make clothes for children; we make them only for women of noble families.'

Knowing how sad I felt, Amma would buy me lace-edged handkerchiefs. I prayed to God that I would grow quickly and soon be able to wear clothes like those the Chinaman had displayed.

The vendor who walked around with a tin trunk that had 'Madame Rose' written on it was a rung below the Chinaman in status. One man carried the trunk and another made the sales. There were frocks that even I could wear. They were not expensive like the Chinaman's silks and they were made of cotton that lasted. Amma bargained with the help of the cook. 'No,' he would say loudly, 'we don't want such costly things,' and disappear. Amma and all of us would go away to our rooms. Left there all by himself, the vendor would fret and call out, 'Come on, I'll lower the prices.' The cook would appear at once and say, 'What! Haven't you left? Master will be back from office now. He'll be furious if he sees hawkers like you hanging around. He'll drive you out. So take your trunk and get out quickly.' Confused and upset, the man would sell us everything very cheap and leave the place. When I wore Madame Rose's dresses to school, I'd feel proud of my figure. Once, the only Tamil girl in my class, Radhamani Swaminathan, said to me, 'Kamala, we're South Indians, both of us. It upsets me when you wear short dresses that show your knees. Can't you wear the kind of clothes I wear?'

Radhamani was three years older than me. She usually wore a skirt and blouse with a half-sari and on festival days she wore a sari. I was not tall enough or rounded enough to wear a sari gracefully. I took great pleasure in calling out to all the hawkers who went walking or cycling through the lane in front of the house. Even though I knew their wares were mediocre, I would ask them to come and sit on the front steps and talk to me. I loved listening to their stories. Narayanan Nair, who ruled our household, disliked my being so friendly with strangers.

'If you call bangle sellers and candy-floss vendors to the house and spend your time talking to them, they'll kidnap you one day. There are places in Calcutta where girls are sold. They say you can get two or three thousand rupees for one.'

'And who will buy children? Those who don't have any?' I asked.

'I don't know how to explain to you. I just can't! But I'll tell you this: if you call all kinds of people here and talk to them like this, it's you who'll suffer. They'll take you away. Your father can scold everyone all he wants, but it won't be any use. Once they kidnap you, the people in your house won't be able take you back.'

The harshness in Narayanan Nair's voice distressed me.

'Why do you say they won't take me back? Why won't my father allow me to stay here if the police bring me back?'

'You'll see! How will they take back a child who's been staying with prostitutes? No one in good families will take a girl like that.' Narayanan Nair's prophesies depressed me. I stopped calling the hawkers home when Parukutty, the servant maid, was not around. Parukutty would say, 'Tell them to give me some sindooram, child. And a good lice-comb.' But none of them had either of these.

'I've so many lice in my hair. If I were in the village, I would make a comb out of bamboo. Have you seen one? You can kill all the lice in your hair in two days. And sleep peacefully afterwards.'

'How did so many lice get into your hair?'

'I don't know, child. My hair attracts them. It's always full of lice that are as big as jackfruit seeds! My thumb is sore from killing them. You're so lucky, child, they never get into your hair. It must be because of the shampoo you use. But shampoo's hot, child. Soon your hair will split and you'll grow bald. You have to use taali leaves if you want your head to feel cool. If you can't get the leaves, you must use green gram ground to a paste.'

'What do you use on your hair, Parukutty?'

'Me? I put by a little rice water at night and use it in the morning before my bath. It doesn't take out all the oil. But that doesn't matter—it's good to have a little oil on one's hair. Otherwise your head turns hot. See how long my hair is . . . below the knees! You can't say it's thin, but it could be a little thicker. When I go back to the village and have a bath in the river, my hair really grows. The tap water here doesn't agree with me. It smells of urine.'

'It must be your bathroom that smells of urine.'

'Oh no, how can that be? I wash the floor twice a day with my broom. It doesn't smell at all. It's the water that comes from the tap that smells. These dirty people must be urinating into the water.'

'Why should they do that?'

'How can I answer that, child? Some people are hard-hearted, that's all. Haven't you heard that when Brahmin women make dosas for Nairs, they rub some spittle on top of each one? For what? To pollute it, that's all. To give others trouble. They take pleasure in that. I don't know, child, I never do despicable things like that.'

'You don't like Calcutta, do you, Parukutty?' I asked.

Parukutty smiled, wrinkling the side of her nose that had a nose ring on it.

'I like it everywhere, whether it's Calcutta or Anandapuram or my own village. All I want is to live in peace somewhere in this world. I'm not at all particular where it is. There are good people and bad people everywhere. What's the point of saying stubbornly that you want to meet only good people? It's God who created bad people too, isn't it? God makes you do good and he makes you commit sins as well. What can we do child—we're only helpless human beings. Can we disobey God?'

'If God asks you to commit a sin, will you do so, Parukutty?' I asked.

'If Guruvayoorappan tells me to, how can I not?'

'Have I committed a sin?'

'How would I know, child? But you're not old enough yet. Once they start having periods, women begin to commit sins . . .'

'How do they commit sins? Will you tell me, Parukutty?'

'Oh, my child, your parents will beat me up and drive me out if I teach you how to commit sins. Don't deprive me of a livelihood, child. Ask me anything else and I'll tell you . . .'

'I don't want to know anything else,' I said firmly.

'What's wrong with this child? Are you mad? Go and study now—your exams are coming. You shouldn't be asking people questions like these.'

When the Hindu–Muslim riots started in Calcutta, we left the house on Lansdowne Road and moved to 15 Lake Avenue. It was situated well away from the main roads. It had a lawn in front and a garden. The kitchen and dining room were upstairs. My study table was placed under the staircase and I slept in the bedroom next to it. From the window, I could see the iron gate and the hawkers that appeared from time to time within its frame. The daughter of the film actress who lived next door and I used to swing on that gate. Her pet name was Babloo. Whenever the man who sold sonpapdi passed that way, Babloo would stop him and buy four annas' worth. She would break the sweet with her dirty nails and hold it out to me and I would refuse to eat it.

'I'm not a Shudra. I'm a Brahmin girl. You can eat what I give you,' she said to me once.

'I know you're a Brahmin too,' she said. I did not have the courage to say I wasn't.

'How did you know?' I asked.

Babloo was swinging on the gate and munching sonpapdi. She screwed up her eyes and smiled. 'Do you think a Shudra girl would have your intelligence?' she asked.

'Wouldn't she?'

'No. It's not intelligence that Shudras need. They need health and strong limbs so that they can work hard,' said Babloo.

'Don't Brahmins need health and strength then?' I asked.

'They need health—to perform pujas, write books and pray. I once suspected that your father was not a Brahmin because he's so dark. But my mother said there are dark Brahmins in South India.'

'My father's not dark. If he were to use make-up like your mother, he'd be as light-skinned as she is!'

She ran back to her house, laughing.

Babloo's mother used to come to our house every day at eleven in the morning to telephone someone. Narayanan Nair would stand behind the curtains and eavesdrop on the conversation which was punctuated by suppressed laughter and groans. Narayanan Nair told me that she was having an affair with a man who was not her husband.

'You must tell your father, child, and stop this foolishness,' he said.

'Let them talk. What do we lose?' I asked.

'So you think we don't lose anything? Let her flirt if she wants to. But in her own house. I don't like her coming here and saying unsavoury things in your hearing. It's your father's money she's spending on telephone! Our telephone is not meant for all sorts of Bengali women to talk to their lovers. Saying silly things and giggling and grunting while a young girl is listening . . . I long to slap her. If I'm given permission, I'll drive her out. I'm not afraid of her. Don't let these Bengalis get too close to you, child. Keep them at a distance. Otherwise they'll be all over you . . . they'll climb on your head and eat up your ears!'

I conjured up the picture of Bengalis climbing up my father's head and eating his ears. I said uneasily, 'You're right. We shouldn't let people get too close . . .'

'You're growing up, child. You're a good child—you understand what people tell you. There's a person here who has no brains at all. There's no use talking to her. How many times I've told her not to stand and talk to those drivers. What's the use? She is always in the garage, grinning from ear to ear. One day they'll catch hold of her, just you see. When she screams for help, there'll be only me to save her. Her mouth waters when she sees a fair skin, the shameless hussy!'

'Who are you talking about?' I asked. Narayanan Nair did not answer.

❖

One day Ammaman said, 'It's not enough to learn to read—you must learn to think.' From that day, Ettan and I made continued efforts to think. Ettan would sit astride the branch on the northern side of the huge mango tree and think. I sat on the swing suspended from the ilanji tree, moved up and down slowly and taught myself to think. While I thought, I saw the trees on the edge of our pond, the bushes of yellow arali and henna, the coconut palms in the burning ground in the southern compound, the fields on the north and the neermathalam tree in the snake shrine. I heard the mantras chanted by the water flowing through the canal from the pond to the field and the messages the south-west wind wafted in through the branches of the kanhira, ilanji and mango trees. I almost felt I could hear the sound of the waves on the distant stretch of the Arabian Sea.

'What are you thinking about?' I would sometimes ask Ettan.

'What are you thinking about, Aami?' he would answer.

I wanted Ettan and me to think about the same thing at the same time.

'I was thinking of the mathematics exam that's around the corner.'

I was astonished, 'I too!' The thought of approaching exams always aggravated my fears about them. While Ettan thought of the prizes and medals he was going to win, I thought of the failures I would face. Mathematics was the subject I found most difficult.

When Ettan left Calcutta and went to Madras to study medicine, I felt really orphaned. No one else ever talked to me openly or encouraged me to talk openly to them. One evening, as I hung on the gate and swung to and fro, Ettan's friend Iswar passed that way.

'Has Mohan written?' he asked.

'Yes,' I said.

'I've bought a new bike. You can sit behind me if you want while I ride around the lake.'

'No, Achan won't like that,' I said.

'No one would think you are a coward, looking at you,' he said, smiling.

'And what would you think I am, looking at me?' I asked.

'A girl with guts.'

Amma was in Kerala at that time. Achan and I had stayed back in Calcutta, with servants to run the house. Maybe because I was alone, I used to be very frightened if there was lightning and thunder at night and if the wind shook the glass shutters of the windows. My only companion was a kitten with white and yellow streaks. I would put it under my blanket and lie awake, listening to it purr. Once, when there was a rumble of thunder, it scratched my shoulder, jumped off the bed, terrified, and ran off to hide somewhere.

Achan had told me long ago that I had to get used to sleeping by myself in my room. He would not allow even a servant maid to sleep there.

'You won't become brave unless you sleep alone,' he would say.

I not only did not become brave but a feeling of insecurity grew within me as time passed. I would arrange a number of books around my pillow and imagine that the people who had written them would stand guard over me when I went to bed. Lord Byron, Isadora Duncan the dancer, Tolstoy: all of them protected me while I slept. In spite of this, ghosts and spirits crept into my room though the moonlight and looked deep into my eyes, scattering strange fears through my langourous mind.

Amma had had an attack of typhoid fever and had gone to Kerala when she recovered. After that, she had been unwilling to return to Calcutta.

Achan said, 'If Amma won't come here, I'll resign and go to Kerala.' He was not even fifty. No Indian held a higher post than Achan did at the time. Anxious not to be a burden to him, I avoided him as much as I could. On the rare occasions he saw me at lunch, he would ask, 'Are you studying hard, Aami? You haven't forgotten, have you, that the exams are nearing?'

I would shake my head meekly.

One evening, Achan came home earlier than usual and saw me dressed in a sari, playing at being grown-up. He looked at me silently for a moment. Then he looked sharply at the handsome young man who was teaching me drawing.

'That's enough of drawing lessons,' said Achan. My drawing classes stopped abruptly.

He had already sent my dance teacher away, saying that I was growing up fast. And the Hindi tutor, saying there was no use learning Hindi. When the drawing teacher was also dismissed, my eyes filled with tears. I lay down on my bed, buried my face in the pillow and cried loudly, 'I don't want to grow up!'

It may have been because I did not get enough attention at home that I became very close at that time to my English teacher, Sneha Laha. She was forty-two. The muscles on her face had slackened with age. In spite of that, I thought her beautiful—the most beautiful of all the beautiful women I had ever seen.

'Miss Laha,' I wrote to her, 'you are like a fresh rose.' When I went to Nalapat for the summer holidays, I wrote poems and letters to her that I could never send, comparing her to a flower. When I told Muthassi about my deep love for my teacher, she said, 'Good! That's better than falling in love with boys.'

Muthassi's greatest fear was that I would marry Byron. He was handsome enough, but a Christian. Although I told her over and over again that he was dead, Muthassi would not believe me. 'You're saying that to comfort me. How can he die? He's so young! I'm sure he's alive somewhere in Calcutta,' she would say, looking at his picture.

Ammamma found out from somewhere that I was writing love poems to my teacher and was distressed.

'Can't you think of anything to write about except love?' she asked, her voice harsh.

'Maybe. But I can't think of anything else now,' I said.

There was a young bhagavathar staying at Ambazhathel house at that time to teach the girls classical music. He was a harmless young man, short, with curly hair. One of his teeth was very wide. When he talked to girls, feigning shyness, displaying his big tooth, Ammamma was afraid I would be attracted to him. He put on the same shy manner with older women and men as well. Indeed he had a perpetually newly wed look about him. This led to Ammamma constantly misunderstanding his intentions.

'There's that bhagavathar! Aami, don't go out,' she would say.

I was irritated with Ammamma. I was used to living in a big city and meeting good-looking men who were rich and fashionable all the time, yet she thought I would fall in love with this meek young man who woke up at dawn every day to practise music. I laughed at her fears.

The music teacher confided in me about the girls who adored him. I did not reveal his secrets to anyone. Maybe it was because I was a bird of passage arriving only in summer that the young man felt he could safely tell me his secrets.

He said to me one day, 'I can tell you're in love, Kamala, just by looking at you.'

I didn't reply.

'And who is the fortunate man? Tell me,' he said, smiling.

'Not a fortunate man—it's a fortunate woman. My class teacher, Sneha Laha.'

Ammamma came running out nervously when the bhagavathar laughed.

Epilogue

I grew up listening to stories: stories that Amma selected from European literature and narrated to me and Ettan, stories the grandmothers used to tell us at dusk from the *Ekadashi Mahatmyam, Bharatam, Bhagavatham* and *Ramayanam,* stories that took shape when Cheriamma recited narrative poems to us, Kumaran Asan's *Nalini, Leela* and *Karuna.* But the anecdotes our servants told us about people who lived in our village and the local gossip they shared with us were what I enjoyed most. The dividing line between truth and fiction would often dissolve as I listened to these stories, laced with humour and passion. The other storytellers spoke of a fictional world, of people who lived very different lives from ours, while the world the servants described was real, earthy and tangible. The vivid characters and events they described peopled my imagination and became part of the experience of growing up.

Much later, when my friend Ramanlal Patel asked me to try to recall my childhood, the voices of these storytellers began to resound in my ears again. I began to fit the fragments of dialogue I gradually recaptured into patterns like one puts together the pieces of a jigsaw puzzle. They provided rich and varied material for my imagination to work with, to extend and enlarge. I discovered that

the world they came from, the world of my own
childhood, remains a treasure-house of memories from
whose inexhaustible depths I can still invoke tale after
wonderful tale . . .

Kinship Terms

Achan: father

Ammaman: mother's brother

Ammamma, Muthassi: mother's mother

Ammayi: Ammaman's wife

Cheriamma: mother's younger sister

Edathi, Oppu: elder sister

Ettan: elder brother

Valiamma: mother's elder sister